BRITANNICA First BIG Book of WHY

BRITANNICA First BIG Book of WHY

Text by Sally Symes and Stephanie Warren Drimmer
Illustrations by Kate Slater

BRITANNICA BOOKS

Contents

MINIBEASTS

PETS

WILD ANIMALS

THE BODY

MINIBEASTS

Why are slugs slimy? And other curious questions about creepy-crawlies

Why do ants live together?

Ants live and work together to help one another survive and thrive. An ant nest is called a colony, and female ants are in charge. They each have a role to play. The queen lays the eggs, sometimes millions of them over her lifetime. The workers, who are all female, find food, clean or look after baby ants. As the colony grows, workers also add new rooms to the nest: nurseries, pantries – even rooms for themselves to take a well-earned rest!

Fire ants weave themselves together to make a life raft in order to escape flooding.

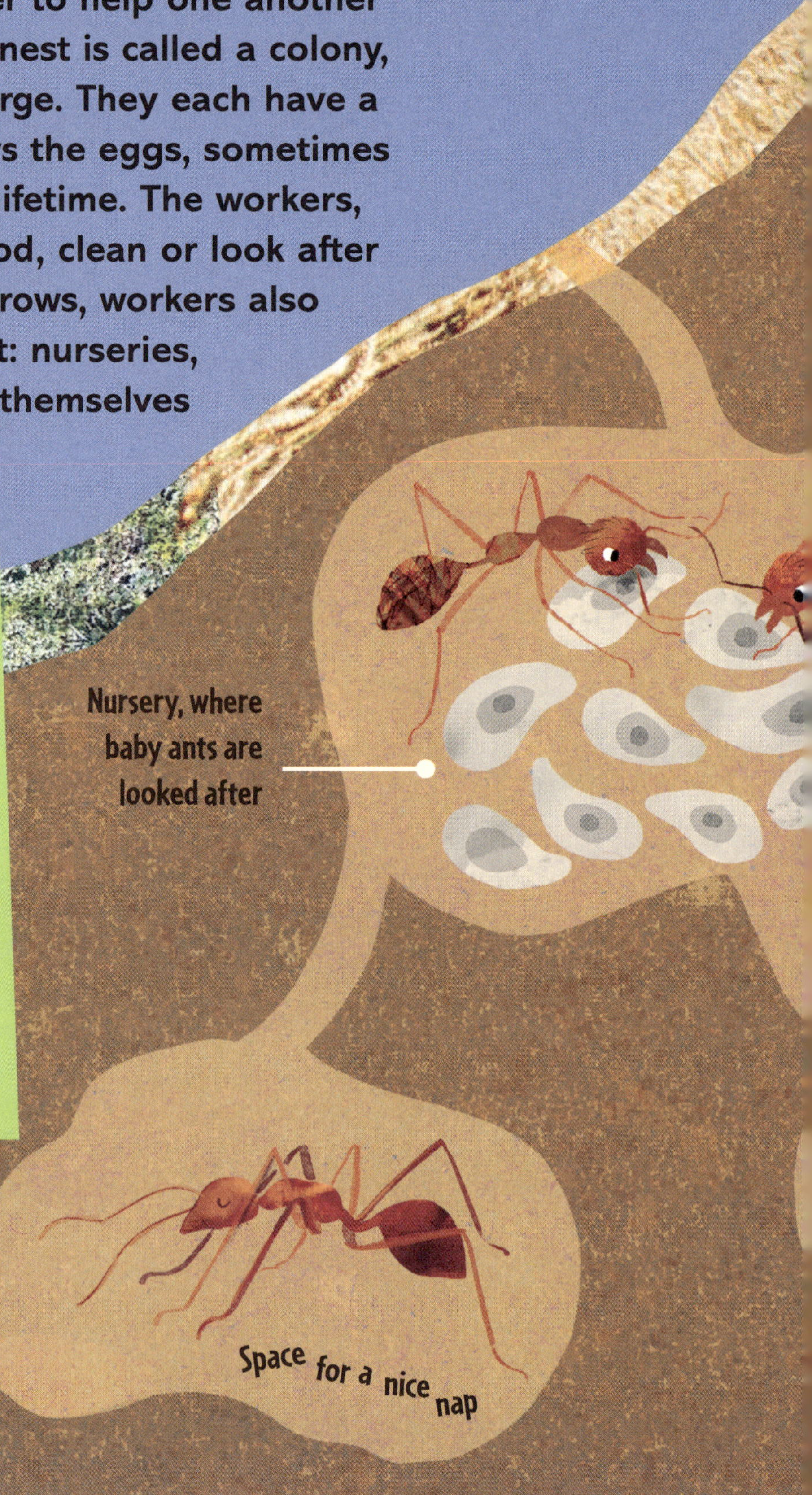

WHO KNOWS?

Ants protect some plants from diseases by releasing a disease-killing substance. Scientists aren't yet sure exactly how this special ant medicine works.

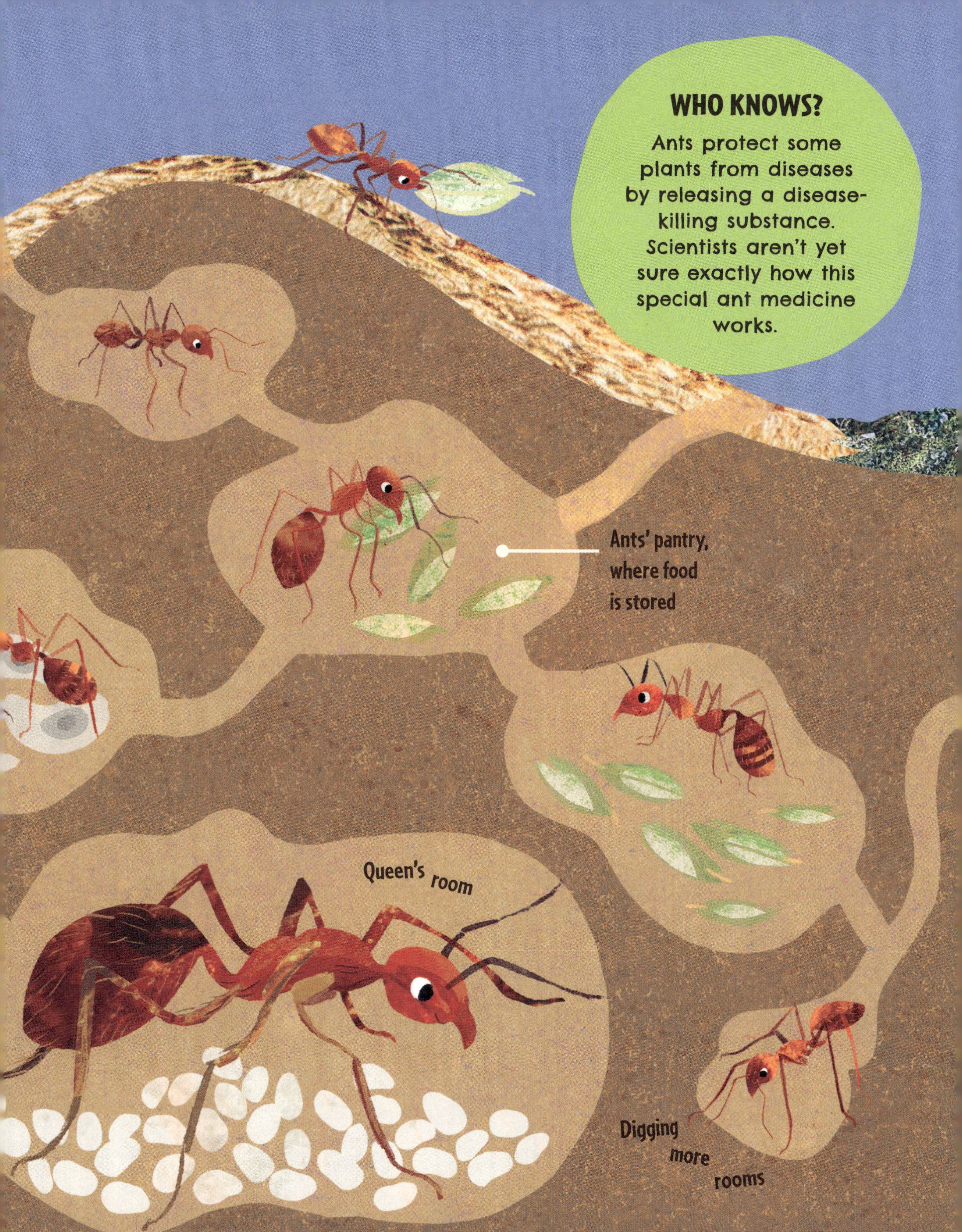

Why do spiders make webs?

Many spiders make webs to catch spider dinners! They build their webs in places where there are lots of juicy insects flying around. As soon as an insect gets tangled, a spider will rush over and inject its prey with a special venom, which stops the insect from moving. The spider then wraps its meal with spider silk, so it's ready to eat later on.

WACKY FACT

Some spiders use their silk to fly. It's called ballooning. They release trails of silk that catch the breeze, taking the spider wherever the wind blows.

Spiders use their back legs to pull silk from special openings on their undersides called spinnerets.

Why do flies like poo?

Houseflies like poo because, to them, it tastes delicious! Flies taste things with their feet. They crawl all over the stinky stuff and spit out special chemicals that transform the poo into juice. Then, flies suck up the juice with their straw-shaped mouths. Slurp! They also lay their eggs in poo so their growing fly babies can get all the food they need.

WACKY FACT

Houseflies like eating poo, and they like to do lots of poos, too! They do a poo every four to five minutes.

Baby flies are called maggots. It takes one or two weeks for the little wrigglers to become flies.

Slurp, slurp

Houseflies have
two huge eyes that
can see nearly all
the way around.

WACKY FACT

If attacked, a centipede can leave a few of its legs in a predator's mouth and escape. The lost limbs will grow back later.

A giant centipede like this one can grow as long as a fork.

Why do centipedes have so many legs?

Centipedes use their legs to run very fast, which makes them excellent hunters! Once they catch their prey, they use the super-flexible tips of their legs like lassos, roping down their victims before injecting them with venom and taking a bite. Where does the venom come from? Well, the first set of a centipede's legs are actually venomous fangs.

This skittery critter is a common house centipede. It's found – you guessed it – in houses!

Why do bees make honey?

Bees spend the summer months collecting sweet nectar from flowers and storing it in honeycombs inside their hives. By the time winter arrives, the liquid nectar has turned into honey. Honeybees need this honey so they have food to eat when it's chilly outside. In the hive, the bees eat the honey and huddle together to keep warm. It's the perfect cold-weather food for hungry bees!

WACKY FACT

The ancient Egyptian king Tutankhamun was buried with a pot of honey. When his tomb was discovered 3,000 years later, the honey was still good enough to eat!

Bees need to visit around two million flowers to make enough honey to fill one jar.

A colony of bees makes far more honey than it needs to survive the winter. Beekeepers can harvest the extra honey without the bees going hungry.

A ladybird's colourful outer shell has two wings underneath. When a ladybird is ready to fly, the shell opens up and the wings unfold.

WACKY FACT

If an animal tries to attack, a ladybird will roll on its back and play dead. If that doesn't work, it spurts stinky, icky yellow blood from its legs.

Why do ladybirds have spots?

In the animal world, bright colours can mean a creature is poisonous. So a ladybird's bright red, spotty body is a warning for predators to keep away. Baby ladybirds have spots, too. Aside from that, they look nothing like their parents. They are long, spiny and black.

A ladybird hatches from its egg as a tiny, spiny larva.

Not all ladybird species are red. They can also be pink, yellow, white, blue, black, orange or even black with red spots. Some have stripes. Others don't have any markings at all!

Why does a caterpillar make a chrysalis?

A caterpillar is a young butterfly. It spends most of its time eating and growing. One day, the caterpillar stops munching, finds somewhere safe to hang and makes a shiny chrysalis. Inside, the caterpillar transforms into a grown-up butterfly.

When it's ready to become an adult, the plump caterpillar hangs under a twig or leaf.

Starting at the head, the caterpillar's striped skin splits upwards to reveal a shiny chrysalis underneath.

The skin drops to the ground, and the soft chrysalis hardens to protect the caterpillar.

WHO KNOWS?

Scientists have discovered caterpillars that love eating plastic bags. They have no idea how they digest the plastic!

The butterfly makes its way out of the chrysalis and flutters away.

After about a week, the caterpillar soup transforms into a butterfly.

Inside its protective chrysalis, the caterpillar's body dissolves into a goopy liquid.

WHO KNOWS?

Worms come to the surface when they feel the vibration of falling rain. No one really knows why, but some experts think it's because worms find it easier to travel across wet soil.

Worms are great for your garden! They churn up the soil, and their waste makes super-pooper plant food.

Why do worms live underground?

Worms need moisture to survive, which is why they spend most of their lives underground where they won't shrivel up under the hot sun. It's a worm wonderland down there: dark, damp and full of delicious dirt to eat. Worms are perfectly suited to life underground: they have tiny bristles all over their bodies that help them to burrow their way through the soil.

Why are slugs slimy?

Slugs need a gunky layer of slime to help them slide smoothly over rough ground. This icky, sticky stuff allows them to climb over objects at any angle – even upside down! The only thing they can't do is go backwards. Slime also protects slugs from drying out in the hot sun and makes them taste absolutely disgusting to predators.

WHO KNOWS?

When threatened, the red triangle slug from Australia spews a super-gluey goo that makes its enemies so sticky they can't move. But scientists don't know how the slug keeps from sticking to itself.

For a quick return to the ground, slugs sometimes use their slime to make a gungy bungee jump.

You may have noticed that slugs don't have legs, but did you know they have a 'foot'? That's the name for their belly.

WACKY FACT

Some snail species use their shells to bash their enemies!

A snail's organs are protected by its shell.

A snail's coiled shell grows bigger as the snail grows bigger.

Why do snails have shells?

Snails are very, very slow. They can't outrun their enemies, but they can certainly disappear quickly... into their shells! A snail's hard shell acts like armour against larger predators that peck. Shells also help snails avoid freezing or drying out in extreme weather. Some snails hibernate by sealing themselves inside their shells with a big glob of mucus.

If small creatures such as ants try to invade their home, snails quickly ooze a bubbly foam to stop them in their tracks.

Why do mosquitoes bite?

Only female mosquitoes bite, and only when they're making babies. The mums-to-be drink blood because they need it to help their eggs develop. But lady mozzies don't bite with teeth. Instead, they use the sharp tip of their tube-like mouths to pierce a creature's skin before taking a good, long slurp.

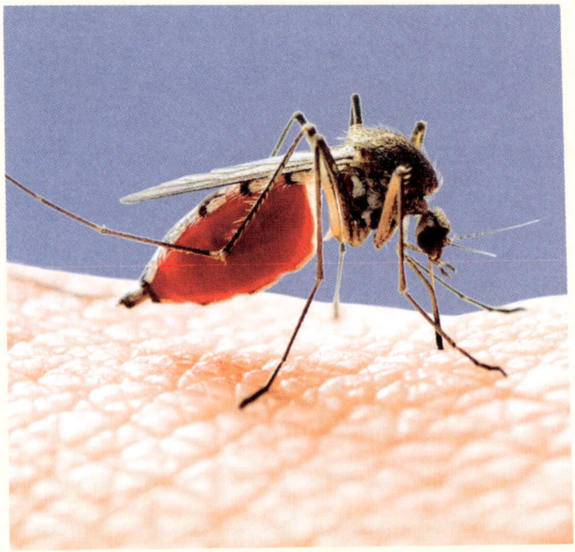

Mosquitoes' tummies grow bigger and redder as they drink.

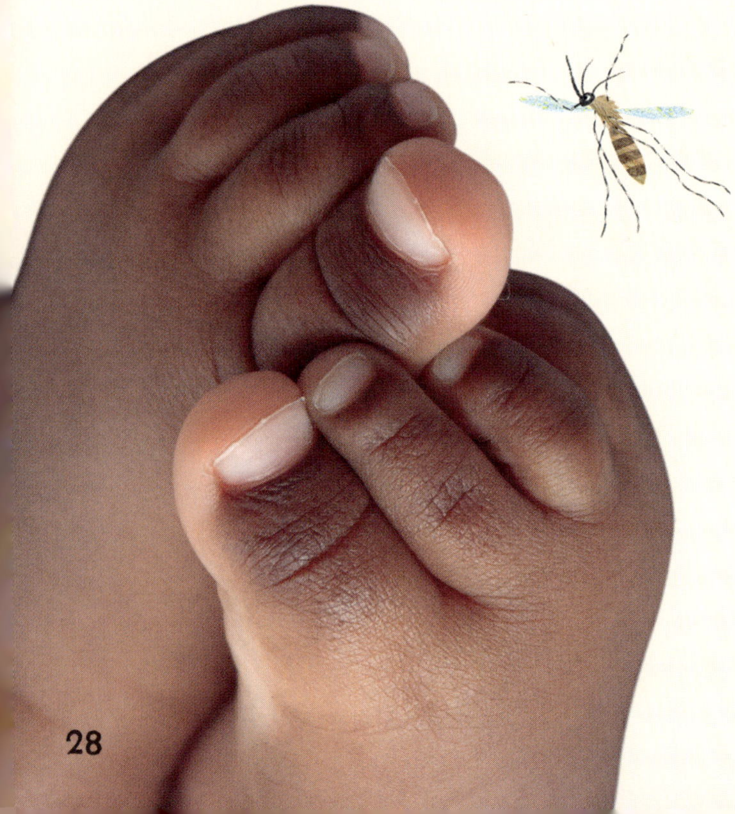

Mosquitoes love toes! They just adore the smell of sweat and bacteria, making toes a bloodsucking hot spot.

WACKY FACT

A mosquito can drink up to three times its weight in blood.

WACKY FACT

Not all fireflies light up. Many species give off smells to attract a mate instead.

Why do fireflies glow?

Fireflies come out on summer nights and light up their bottoms as a way to locate each other. Here's how it works: as he flies, a male firefly switches on and off like a tiny torch, hoping that a female will take a fancy to him. If a female likes his flashing pattern, she'll flash back.

Each species of firefly has a unique blinking pattern that attracts only its own kind. Firefly glows can be yellow, green, orange or even blue!

Why are praying mantises so hard to see?

Praying mantises are masters of disguise. The colour and shape of their bodies blend in perfectly with their leafy surroundings, making them very tricky to spot. This allows praying mantises to sneak up on prey without being noticed. They can also hide from predators that want to eat them for dinner!

Orchid mantises are also great at disguising themselves. They trick their insect prey into thinking they are a flower that's safe to land on.

A praying mantis keeps very still until a juicy insect comes near. Then it quickly shoots out its spiky front legs, grabs the insect and gobbles it up.

WACKY FACT

Praying mantises have only one ear, and it's on their chests.

WACKY FACT

When the weather gets cold, stink bugs find a warm place to snuggle down. Then they send out a smell that tells their stinky friends to join them.

Why do stink bugs stink?

Stink bugs look like warriors, with their shield-shaped bodies and armour-like shells. But while the hard shells do help protect them, these tough little bugs have an even better way to stop predators. They make a big stink! If attacked, their bodies release a waxy liquid. It smells so bad that it makes almost all creatures run away.

Stink bugs love to eat fruit and can cause terrible damage to crops.

Wow! What's that?

Here are some bugs with funky 'faces'. Can you match each one to its name?

Answers on page 271

Peacock spider

Blue damselfly

Owl butterfly

Man-faced stink bug

Swallowtail caterpillar

Hawaiian happy-face spider

PETS

Why do cats purr? And other curious questions about our animal friends

Why do dogs sniff each other's bottoms?

A dog's sense of smell is up to 100,000 times better than a human's. Dogs use their noses to explore. One whiff with their super-sniffer gives dogs lots of information. By sniffing, a dog can find out how old, how healthy and how friendly the other dog is. So, when one dog sniffs another dog's bum, it's getting to know its new friend. Sniffing is also how dogs say hello!

WACKY FACT

A dog can detect two different smells at a time – one with each nostril.

Dogs' noses have smell-detecting cells. Dogs with longer noses have more of these cells, so they are better at smelling than dogs with shorter noses.

Cats purr as they breathe in and as they breathe out.

Why do cats purr?

WHO KNOWS?

Cats will usually stop purring when they hear running water. No one really knows why.

A cat purrs when the muscles in its voice box move quickly, causing the diaphragm – a muscle at the base of its chest – to move. When a cat breathes, air touches these moving muscles and a purr comes out. Cats purr for lots of reasons. They purr when they are feeling happy, when they are feeling worried or when they are in pain. Some cats even mix a purr with a miaow to tell you they're hungry.

Mother cats purr when they give birth. Newborn kittens can't see or hear, but they can feel mum's purrs. The kittens purr back.

Why do cats and dogs have claws?

Most animals with legs also have claws. They come in handy for climbing, digging, attacking, defending and getting a grip on stuff – especially food. Claws come in all shapes and sizes. Dogs' thick, stumpy claws make sturdy digging tools and stop them from slipping as they run. Razor-sharp cat claws are great for catching things and for climbing up trees!

WACKY FACT

A cat's claws grow in layers, like an onion. The layers shed about every three months, revealing a new claw underneath.

Cats and dogs have a thumb-like 'dewclaw' higher up on each of their front paws. They use them to grip objects and to steady themselves when running around corners.

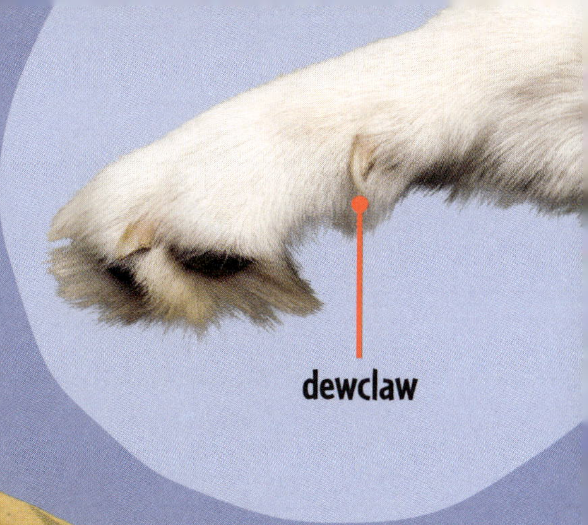

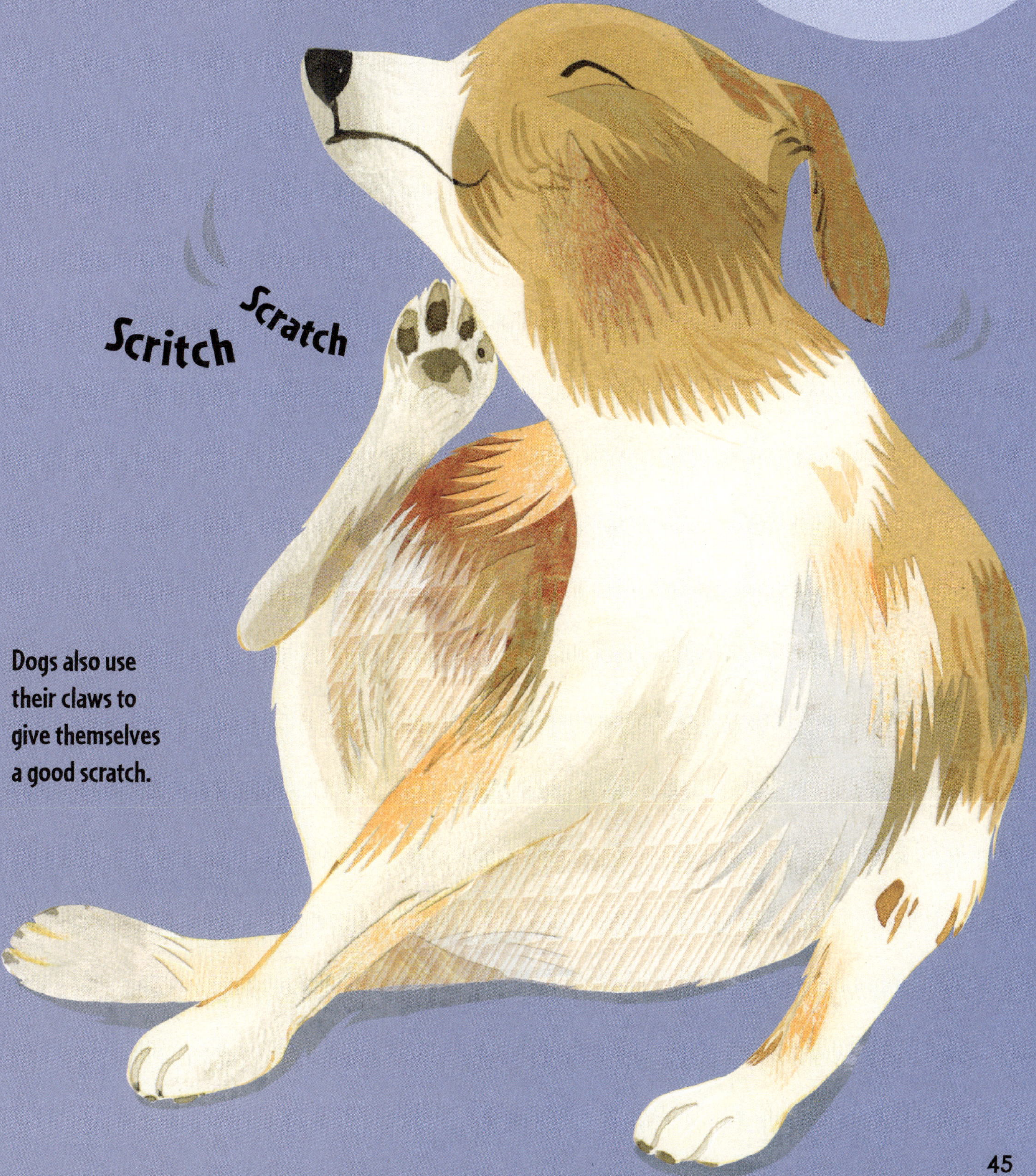

Dogs also use their claws to give themselves a good scratch.

WHO KNOWS?

Experts aren't sure when humans first started taking rabbits from the wild. The earliest rabbit hutches ever discovered are 2,000 years old.

Rabbits can turn their ears almost all the way around.

Why do rabbits have big ears?

Rabbits' big ears do a lot more than just listen for bunny friends or foes – they are essential tools for keeping cool! Rabbits can't sweat, so when their furry bodies get too hot, they release the excess heat through their ears. The ears' supersized surface allows more room for the heat to escape. This is why rabbits who live in hot places tend to have the largest ears.

Lops are a breed of rabbit that have droopy ears. They can't hear as well as their straight-eared bunny buddies.

Why do tortoises walk so slowly?

Tortoises are rarely in a hurry – they have nothing to hurry for. They don't need to chase their food (plants don't have legs), and why bother running away from predators when you have a rock-hard shell to hide in? In fact, tortoises don't often walk on their thick legs. They prefer to slide themselves forwards by pushing with their back legs.

A group of tortoises is called a creep.

WACKY FACT

It's not just their shell that weighs them down. A tortoise's HUGE bladder can hold wee weighing up to nearly half its body weight.

Tortoises live a VERY long time – from 90 to 150 years!

WHO KNOWS?

Golden hamsters are the most popular breed of pet hamster, but there are fewer and fewer of them in the wild. Scientists don't know how many remain in their sandy home near the Syrian city of Aleppo.

Why are hamsters so noisy at night?

Hamsters are nocturnal, which means they snooze during the day and scamper around at night. In the wild, they live in places where it's too hot to be out in the daytime. Wild hamsters sleep in burrows by day to escape the sizzling sun and avoid being eaten by hungry predators.

Hamsters use their special cheek pouches to carry food back to their nests. Some hammy-mums use them to carry their babies, and others fill them with air so they can float on water.

Why are there so many kinds of dogs?

Dogs come in all shapes and sizes: big, small, chunky or slim. The reason they're all so different is because of us – humans! Yes, once we realised how useful our furry companions could be, we had dogs produce puppies in order to raise them for specific jobs. For instance, quick dogs were bred for hunting, clever dogs for herding and big, fierce dogs for guarding and protecting.

WACKY FACT

Chihuahuas are one of the smallest dog breeds. They are about the same height as a pencil.

The tallest dog ever recorded was a Great Dane like this one. He was the same size as a donkey.
Hungarian Puli dogs are used to herd sheep. Their woolly coats make them look a lot like sheep, too!

WACKY FACT

Lungfish can breathe both in and out of water. These strange, slithery creatures can survive for five years on land!

Why do fish have gills?

Just like people, fish need to take in a gas called oxygen in order to live. We get oxygen from the air we breathe, but fish get oxygen from the water. They breathe by using special body parts on the sides of their heads called gills. Gills need water in order to stay open. Without water, gills collapse and the fish can't survive.

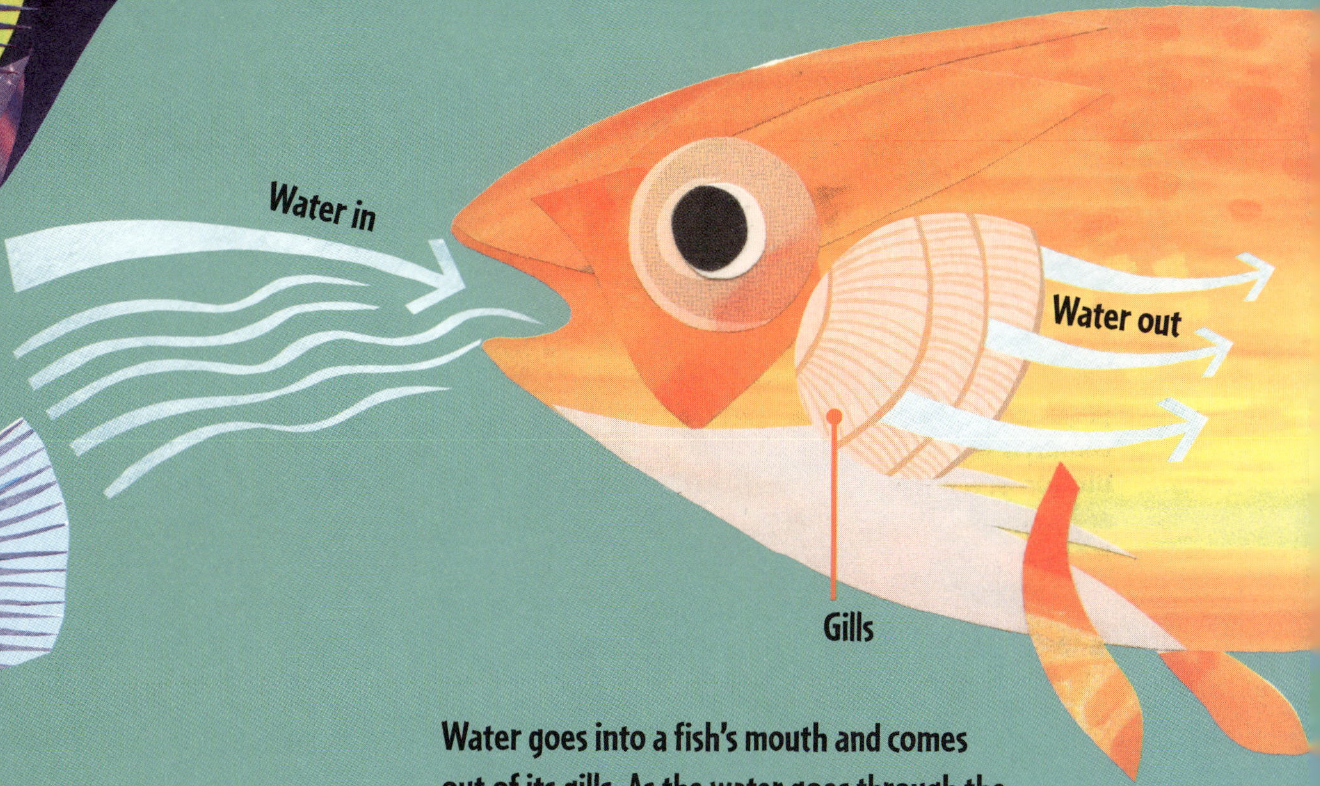

Water goes into a fish's mouth and comes out of its gills. As the water goes through the gills, oxygen is taken into the fish's body.

Why can't animals talk to us?

Only humans speak human languages, but certain pets do understand some human words. Animals mainly communicate by using sounds, body language and smells. Dogs woof and wag their tails when they want our attention. Cats miaow and nuzzle us when they want to be fed. And guinea pigs make a 'wheek-wheek' sound, often accompanied by a 'popcorn' jump when they are excited!

An African grey parrot named Alex was trained to say more than 100 words. He knew some colours and shapes and could even count.

WACKY FACT

Most dogs can understand more than 150 words. That's the same as a two-year-old human.

Rats move their whiskers super fast – they can sweep them to-and-fro seven times a second. That's more than any other whiskered mammal.

WACKY FACT

Humans are one of the few warm-blooded creatures that don't have whiskers.

Why do some animals have whiskers?

Whiskers are long, thick and twitchy hairs that stick out from around the noses and mouths of some animals. Animals use their whiskers a bit like we use our hands and fingers – to touch and explore their surroundings. Rats rely on their supersensitive whiskers more than their eyes to explore the world. They sweep them back and forth constantly in a behaviour called 'whisking'.

Those lovely, long lashes above a cat's eyes are actually whiskers. Cats also have whiskers on the back of their front legs.

Why do cats lick their fur?

Adult cats spend about half of their waking life grooming. They spend hours licking their fur clean with their sandpaper-rough tongues. Cats' tongues are covered with thousands of tiny hooked spikes called papillae. They act like a fine comb to remove dirt, loose hairs and pesky insects such as fleas. Licking also spreads out skin oil, which keeps their fur soft and shiny and helps seal it against cold and damp weather.

WACKY FACT

Cats give themselves a good lick after eating to get rid of food smells. Being odour-free helps them sneak up on prey without being detected.

Cats lick their kitty friends to show affection. They may even groom their human if they like them enough!

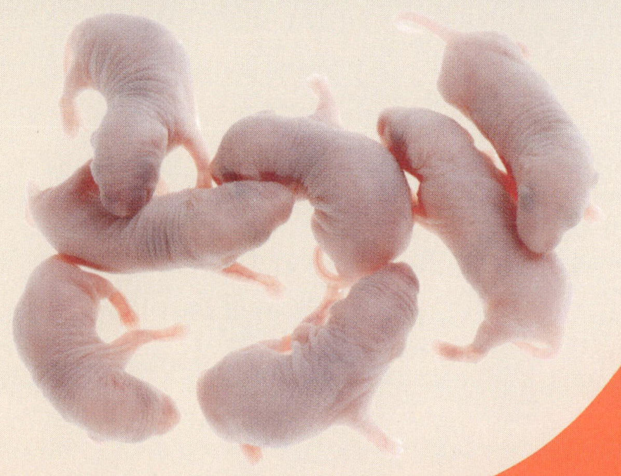

A male mouse is called a 'buck', a female mouse is called a 'doe' and a baby mouse is called a 'pinky'.

Mice have poor eyesight, but excellent senses of smell and hearing.

Why do mice squeak?

Mice have their own squeaky language, which they use to communicate. They make different squeaks depending on how they are feeling and to let their friends know where to find food and water. Some mouse squeaks are too high for humans to hear. Females use high-pitched squeaks to chat to each other, and males sing chirpy love songs to impress the females.

WACKY FACT

Scientists have discovered that, as well as speaking by squeaking, mice also use facial expressions to show their feelings.

Why do gerbils chew cardboard?

Gerbils have long, sharp front teeth that never stop growing. They have to keep chewing to wear them down. In the wild, gerbils chew on tree roots, but pet gerbils chew on household items such as plain cardboard egg boxes and toilet rolls. Cardboard rolls also make cool tunnels to play in, and once shredded, the little nibblers use the pieces to sleep on.

Gerbils are rodents. Guinea pigs, hamsters, rats and mice are rodents, too.

WACKY FACT

Gerbil teeth are hard as iron, and they need to be. In the wild, gerbils use them to nip enemies, open tough nuts and shred wood for sleeping material.

Horseshoes are made in a U-shape to fit neatly over a horse's hooves.

Why do horses need shoes?

Horse hooves are thick, and just like our nails, they are always growing. Trotting about on hard surfaces wears hooves down faster than they can grow, so horses need special shoes to protect their feet. Horseshoes are usually made from hard metal by a person called a farrier. The farrier nails horseshoes to a horse's hooves. But don't worry, it doesn't hurt!

WACKY FACT

Nearly 2,000 years ago, the Romans made special leather shoes called 'hipposandals' to protect their horses' hooves. (Here, 'hippo' means horse, not hippopotamus.)

Hipposandals were made of iron. They were cupped around a horse's hoof, and fastened using leather straps.

Wow! What's that?

Here are some animal friends. Can you match each one to its name?

Answers on page 271

Bubble eye goldfish

Sphynx cat

Bloodhound

Hairless guinea pig

Angora rabbit

Stick insect

WILD ANIMALS

Why do giraffes have long necks? And other curious questions about cool creatures

Why do frogs croak?

It's mainly male frogs who make all the noise. They croak to attract female frogs and to warn other males to stay away. If attacked, some frogs croak to frighten off their enemies. They also croak to warn their froggy friends of danger. Females find male croaking very attractive. They may even join a froggy chorus and sing to a male whose croak they particularly like.

WACKY FACT

The tiny coqui frog from Puerto Rico is about the size of a hazelnut. It's as noisy as an electric food mixer!

This male tree frog sings his croaky love songs at night.

Most frogs have vocal sacs at the bottom of their mouths, which they fill with air. These inflatable chins make their croaks sound even louder.

WACKY FACT

Sharks don't need to use toothpaste! The outside of their teeth is made of fluoride, a mineral that helps keep teeth strong.

Why do sharks have so many teeth?

Sharks wouldn't be as powerful without their teeth. They need them to rip and tear up fishy flesh. But sharks' teeth are pretty wobbly. So all that ripping and tearing means they lose a few teeth with every meal. But that's no problem. Sharks have 15 to 50 rows of teeth arranged in layers. When one tooth falls out, another simply slides into its place. Sharks lose and grow more than 20,000 teeth over a lifetime.

A bull shark like this one can have up to 350 teeth.

Sharks' teeth are arranged in layers inside their large jaws.

Why do crocodiles have bumpy skin?

Crocodiles have tough skin, a bit like armour, to protect them from enemy bites and to stop them from drying out. But that's not all. Look closely and you'll see that crocs have thousands of small black bumps on their lumpy skin. These bumps are even more sensitive than your fingertips. In still water, a crocodile's skin can detect the vibrations of a wildebeest drinking from 20 metres away.

WACKY FACT

Despite their tough appearance, crocs have a soft side. They occasionally give each other an affectionate rub!

A crocodile's hard, bony scales are called scutes. Crocs have thousands of scutes covering their bodies.

The giant Pacific octopus has more than 2,200 suckers!

Why do octopuses have suckers on their arms?

The octopus's eight long, flexible arms are covered with suckers that can touch, taste and smell. The suckers also help them to grasp prey and grip surfaces. And because every supersensitive arm has a brain of its own, each one can act independently. So while two arms crawl along the seabed, the others can be searching in rocky crevices for food.

WHO KNOWS?

If threatened, octopuses can instantly change colour to blend in with their surroundings. But scientists think octopuses can't see colour with their eyes, so they aren't sure how these creatures know what colour to change to.

Why do elephants have trunks?

An elephant needs its trunk for all sorts of things. This amazing swinging tool clings, breathes, smells, sucks, spurts, touches – and even trumpets! But a trunk's main purpose is for eating and drinking. Bending down or reaching high is tricky with a big, bulky body. So an elephant uses its nimble trunk to gather food and suck up water, which it then puts or squirts in its mouth.

WACKY FACT

African elephants have two 'fingers' on the ends of their trunks that allow them to pick up small objects. They can even crack open tiny peanuts.

An elephant's super-schnozzle can smell water up to 19 kilometres away.

Elephants also use their trunks as snorkels.

Joeys stay in their mum's pouch for about four months before taking their first hop-about outside. They're about ten months old when they leave the pouch for good.

WACKY FACT

Very young baby joeys wee and poo in the pouch, so the kanga-mum must regularly lick the pouch clean.

Why do kangaroos have pouches?

Only female kangaroos have pouches. The pouch is a snuggly, safe place for a baby kangaroo. A baby kangaroo is called a joey. It's blind when it's born and looks a bit like a pink jelly bean with legs. Right after birth, the tiny joey crawls up and into its mother's pouch where it drinks her milk and grows big, strong and bouncy.

A joey is born after developing for about 33 days in its mother's womb.

A newborn joey's forelegs are just strong enough to pull it through its mother's fur to the safety of her pouch.

Here, it prepares to drink its mother's milk. Newborns can't swallow, so the mother uses her muscles to pump the milk into the joey's throat.

Why do birds make nests?

Most birds build nests as cosy, sheltered places to keep their eggs and chicks safe. Some build their nests with small sticks, grass and moss. Others use mud and even stones. Hummingbirds make their walnut-sized nests out of flower petals and spider silk!

The sides of a hummingbird's tiny nest stretch like elastic as the babies grow.

WACKY FACT

A bald eagle nest is made from sticks and grass. It can weigh as much as a small car, and it's as wide as one, too.

To scare their rivals, male gorillas stand up tall, roar loudly and beat their chests with open hands (not fists). The boom-boom sound can be heard nearly 2 kilometres away!

Why do gorillas beat their chests?

Gorillas are generally calm, laid-back apes, but if the biggest and strongest male in a group stands up and starts to beat his chest – scram! He's warning other males that he's in charge and will attack if they don't stay away. A female gorilla will beat her chest if she's cross with another female, or if a youngster is getting on her nerves.

WACKY FACT

Even baby gorillas pound their chests sometimes.

Why do snakes flick their tongues?

Snakes smell things using their mouths. To do this, a snake flicks its forked tongue in and out. The tongue collects smells from the air around it. The snake then presses its tongue against a supersensitive place inside its mouth which absorbs the smells, and this is how the snake works out if there's an enemy, a meal or a mate nearby.

WHO KNOWS?

Scientists have discovered that humans can also detect smells with their tongues. They are still trying to find out how this tongue-smelling affects the way we taste food.

A snake picks up smells on both sides of its forked tongue. If one side captures more, that's the direction the smell is coming from.

Snakes stick their tongues out through a little notch in their lips.

WACKY FACT

The feathers under a flamingo's wings are black. You can see them when the birds are flying.

Why are flamingos pink and orange?

Flamingos are born a rather dull grey. But they turn pink or orange because of what they eat. They gobble up algae, larvae and shrimp, which contain carotene, a chemical that turns things an orangey pink colour. When flamingos absorb this carotene, their feathers and skin become colourful.

Flamingos feed with their heads upside down. Their beaks and tongues are able to separate out their food from the mud and water.

Why do squirrels bury nuts?

Food is difficult to find in the winter, so squirrels prepare by burying their food under leaves or in the hollows of trees. They remember these hiding places, returning to dig up their nutty treasures when they're hungry. Some nuts get left behind and grow into trees.

WACKY FACT

If one squirrel thinks another squirrel might try to steal its food, it will sometimes play a trick. It will pretend to drop the nut in a hole, but secretly keep the nut in its mouth.

Squirrels can smell food under 30 centimetres of snow. They begin to dig, following the scent until they find their meal.

Why do owls have big eyes?

Most owls hunt at night, so they need to see in the dark to catch animals to eat. Luckily, their supersized eyes are specially designed to take in extra light, which gives them excellent night vision. And unlike other birds, who have eyes on either side of their heads, owls have both eyes on the front of their face. This makes them better at figuring out how far away their prey is and how fast it is moving. So owls are extremely good at catching their dinner.

WACKY FACT

If a great horned owl like this one were the size of a human, its eyes would be as big as tennis balls!

Owls can't swivel their eyes from left to right, like humans can. But because they have flexible necks, owls can turn their heads almost all the way around.

Why do giraffes have long necks?

A giraffe's long neck allows it to reach leaves in tall trees that shorter creatures can't get to. This means giraffes don't have to compete with other animals for food in the grasslands where they live. Another huge advantage of being head and shoulders above the rest is that giraffes can see predators coming from very far away.

A giraffe's neck is about the same length as its legs.

Giraffes travel together in groups. A group of giraffes is called a tower.

WHO KNOWS?

We don't know for sure, but some scientists think that a giraffe's long neck helps keep it cool by allowing heat to escape from its body.

Penguins have blubbery fat and layers of special feathers to keep them warm in icy water.

When penguins swim it looks a bit like they're flying – but underwater!

Why can't penguins fly?

Penguins aren't built for flight. Their wings are too stiff and stumpy, and their bodies are too heavy. But being hefty and smooth with flipper-like wings makes them really good at something else – swimming! In fact, penguins spend most of their lives in water because that's where their food lives. They can swim faster and dive deeper than any other bird, making them amazing hunters.

WACKY FACT

Rockhopper penguins spend so much time in the sea that some have been found with barnacles like these growing on their feathers.

Wow! What's that?

Here are some curious creatures. Can you match each one to its name?

Answers on page 271

Cassowary

Dumbo octopus

Thorny devil

Peacock mantis shrimp

Sloth

Tarsier

THE BODY

Why does music make me want to dance? And other curious questions about the human body

Why do I yawn?

We all yawn, but nobody is sure about the reason why. We yawn when we wake up, when we're bored or anxious and especially when we're – yaaaaaaawn – tired! Some scientists think we yawn because we need more air or our lungs need a stretch. Others think yawns cool us down and make us more alert. Whatever the reason, we do know this – once somebody yawns, we can't help yawning, too.

People yawn about 20 times a day. Each face-stretching, face-scrunching super-sigh lasts about six seconds.

Once you start a yawn, it's really hard to stop.

WACKY FACT

Animals yawn, too. Dogs often join in if they see their owners yawn!

Children have about 10,000 taste buds on their tongues.

Why does my mouth water?

The watery stuff in your mouth is called saliva (or spit). As you chomp and chew on your food, the saliva helps to turn the food into a slushy, mushy pulp that is easy for you to swallow. When you see, smell or even just think about tasty food, your brain sends a signal to your mouth to release the saliva – so that you are ready to eat!

WACKY FACT

Our mouths ooze more than a litre of saliva a day. That's about the same as four cups.

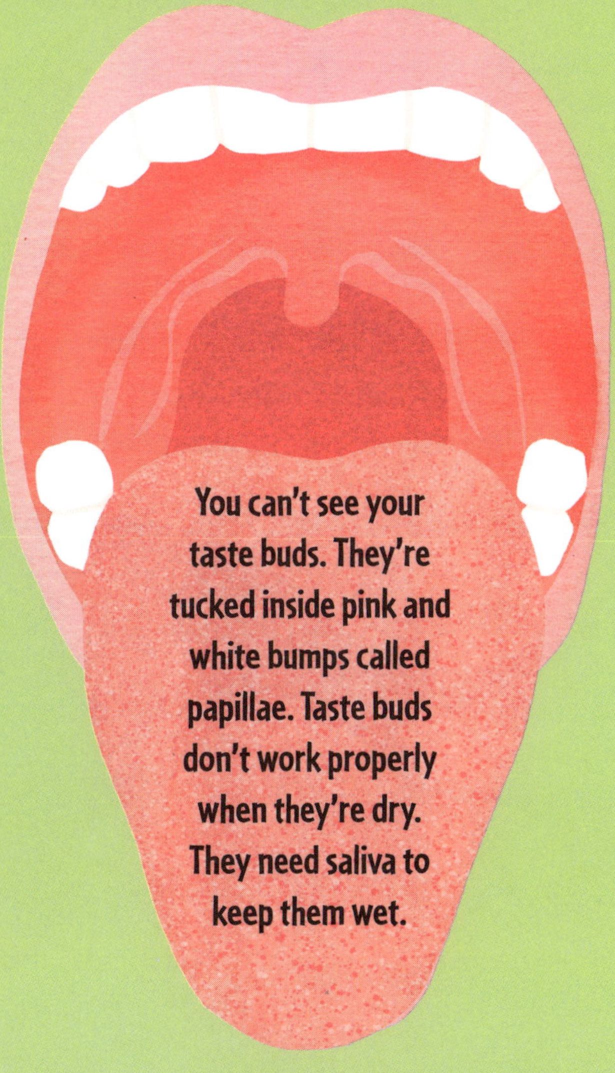

Why do I have wobbly teeth?

You need your teeth to bite and chew food. When you're little, you have room for 20 baby teeth in your mouth. Around the age of six, these teeth begin to wobble and fall out. They get pushed out as bigger grown-up teeth grow in. By the time you are an adult, you'll likely have 32 big teeth.

WACKY FACT

Teeth start growing before you're even born. They're lurking beneath the surface of those baby gums.

Just like people, cats and dogs lose their baby teeth. They have all their grown-up chompers by the time they are six months old.

The most common eye colour in the world is brown.

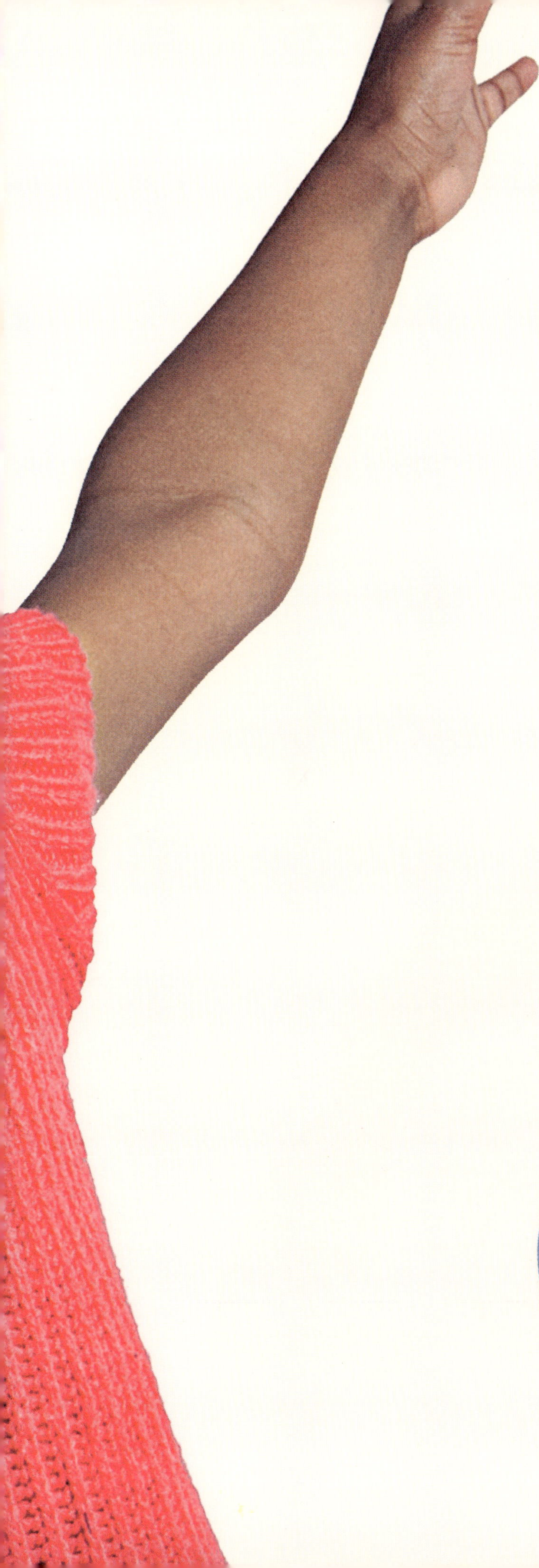

Why do some of us wear glasses?

Not everyone's eyes work in the same way. Some people can see things close-up, but they have trouble seeing things that are far away, such as their friend across the street. Others may see things clearly in the distance, but close-up things look fuzzy. Glasses correct the way eyes work, so whatever is blurry becomes clear.

WACKY FACT

You blink about 15 times every minute. (Bet you just blinked!)

Why do some things make me cry?

You might cry if you are sad, hurt, angry or happy. Strong feelings cause your brain to send a message to your eyes to make tears. Scientists think crying may be a signal to other people that we need help. Tears also keep your eyes clean and healthy, washing away dirt when you blink. Most land animals make tears for this reason, but only humans cry.

WHO KNOWS?

Moths in the Amazon rainforest have been seen drinking the tears of birds. Experts are not quite sure why they do it.

Babies cry to get attention. They may need a nappy changed or food or even a cuddle.

No matter how much we cry, we will never run out of tears!

You are more likely to remember a dream if you wake up in the middle of it.

Why do I dream?

You may not remember your dreams, but you have up to seven every night. Scientists aren't sure why we dream. They think the brain might use dreams to tidy up all the information it has taken in during the day. Happy feelings, worries, things we've seen, heard, touched, tasted and smelled get sorted. As they do, the brain makes pictures and stories out of them.

WHO KNOWS?

Dogs often give a little whimper and twitch their legs when they are having doggie dreams. Scientists think animals dream about their daily activities, but they're not totally sure.

Why do I have eyelashes?

Short, straight, curly or long, you have eyelashes for one purpose – to protect your eyes. Lashes sweep away dust and dirt and warn you to shut your eyes if something touches them. They stop rain and sweat from dripping into your eyes, and they also stop your peepers from drying out on windy days.

WACKY FACT

Camels have two rows of eyelashes to keep the dust and sand out of their eyes in their desert homes.

You have about 150 lashes on your upper lids and about 100 on your lower lids.

WACKY FACT

Skin is the human body's biggest organ. It covers and protects everything inside.

Why is skin different colours?

Human skin produces melanin, a substance that protects your skin from the sun. The more melanin you have, the darker your skin is. Different amounts of melanin in skin produce a range of amazing human skin colours.

Why do I need to brush my teeth?

Did you know your teeth are as strong as shark teeth and that you can keep them that strong by brushing? When you eat, little bits of food get left behind. This food attracts plaque – a clear, yucky coating that sticks to your teeth. Plaque contains germs that can eat small holes in your teeth. Brushing removes food and plaque, and keeps your teeth healthy and sparkling clean!

WACKY FACT

Crocodiles get their teeth cleaned regularly by plover birds. The birds use their sharp beaks to remove bits of meat from between a croc's teeth.

The part of the tooth you can see is called a crown. The rest of the tooth is below the gums.

WHO KNOWS?

Small babies respond to music more than they do to speech. Scientists don't fully understand why, but humans may be born with a built-in desire to dance.

Why does music make me want to dance?

When we hear music, it has a powerful effect on our brain and our emotions. A tune with a fast, strong rhythm switches on the part of your brain that helps you move. You might want to wiggle your toes and jiggle your hips! And guess what? Listening and dancing to music causes your brain to release chemicals that make you feel super happy!

Humans have been creating music for thousands of years. The flutes illustrated here are made from bird wing bones. They were carved around 8,000 years ago, and can still be played.

Why does my tummy rumble?

Inside your tummy are your intestines, a long winding tube that removes all the things the body needs from food, such as vitamins, so your body can use them. The intestines squish and squeeze anything leftover, and they're rumbling all the time. When you're hungry, your stomach makes even more rumbly noises. It's sweeping away any leftover bits of food, so it's clean and empty and ready for your next meal.

WACKY FACT

When we eat and drink, we also swallow air, which is a gas. Most food and drinks contain gases, too. All these gases gurgle and bubble up and pop out as a

burp!

Rumble-rumble!
Squish!
Squelch!

WHO KNOWS?

Most hiccups go away after a few minutes. If they don't, people sometimes hold their breath for a few seconds. Scientists aren't sure why, but this trick sometimes stops the hiccups.

Why do I get hiccups?

Hiccups can happen if you eat or drink something too quickly. Being super excited or having a laughing fit can also be triggers. These things upset a dome-shaped muscle at the bottom of your chest called the diaphragm. Your diaphragm helps you breathe in and out. It normally works perfectly, but when it's irritated, it gets twitchy, making you breathe in quick, little gasps. As the air rushes in, it causes you to hiccup!

The word 'hiccup' sounds like the noise it makes, doesn't it? It's fun to say in other languages, too: *hoquet* (French), *hikke* (Norwegian), *hazuq* (Arabic), *hiksti* (Icelandic) and *hicakī* (Punjabi).

Why do some people have curly hair and others have straight hair?

Like a plant, each of your hairs has a root. You can't see it because it's hidden just beneath your skin. The root is inside a tiny tube called a follicle. The hair grows up the follicle and out through the skin where you can see it. Follicles can be different shapes. Whether you have straight, curly or wavy hair depends on the shape of your follicles.

WACKY FACT

Your hair can't feel pain – or anything else for that matter! This is because hairs don't have any nerves, the cells that carry our sense of touch.

A follicle is hollow, like a drinking straw. If you look down at a follicle from above, you can see its shape. This is what determines whether you have curly, straight or wavy hair.

Curly hair comes from a follicle that is oval in shape.

Straight hair comes from a round follicle.

Wavy hair comes from a follicle that is squashed in on one side.

WACKY FACT

Your nails (and hair) are made out of keratin. It's the same substance that dinosaur claws were made of!

Why do I have nails?

Nails stop the ends of your fingers and toes from being squashed every time you touch or tread on something. They also help protect your supersensitive fingers and not quite so supersensitive toes from injuries. And nails act as tools. They help with stuff like peeling stickers, picking fluff off clothes and scratching itches.

If you didn't cut your fingernails for a year, they would measure about the same length as a paper clip.

Wow! What's that?

Here are some pictures showing parts of the human body. Can you match each one to its name?

Answers on page 271

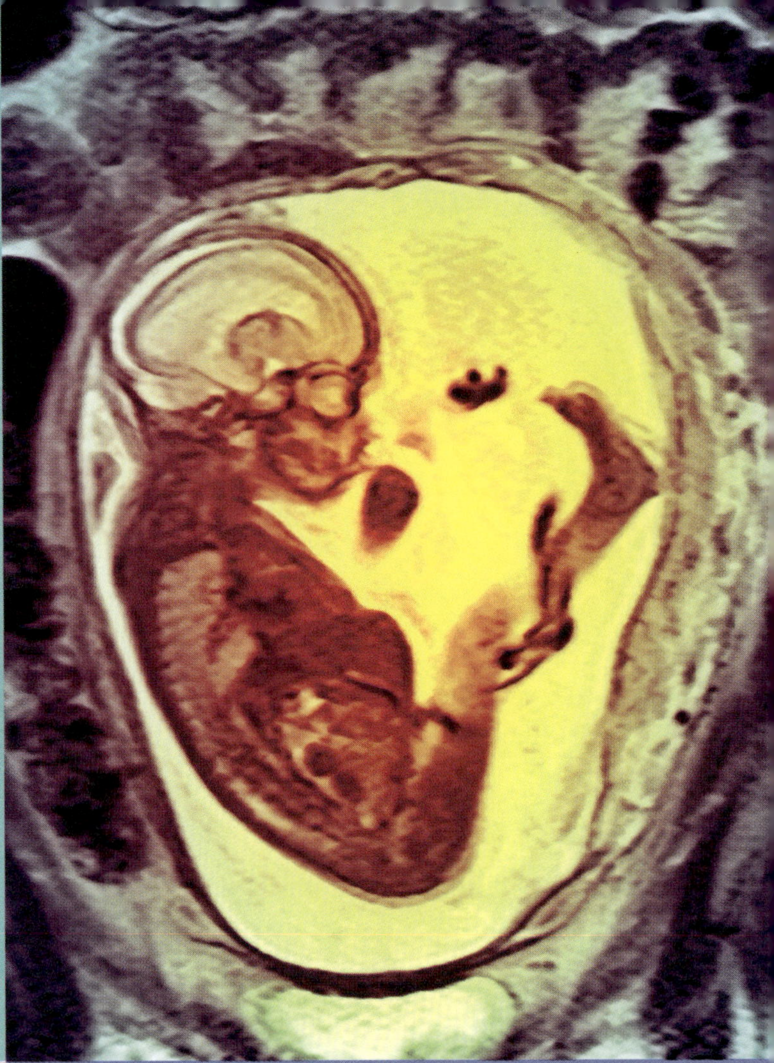

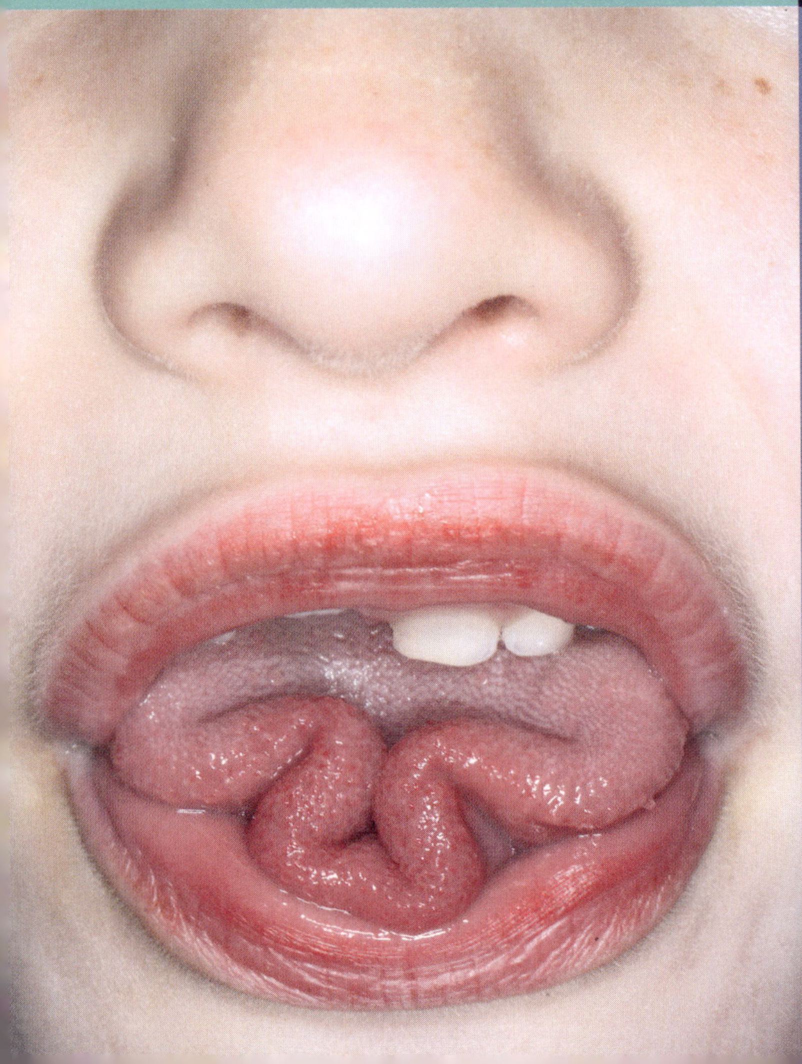

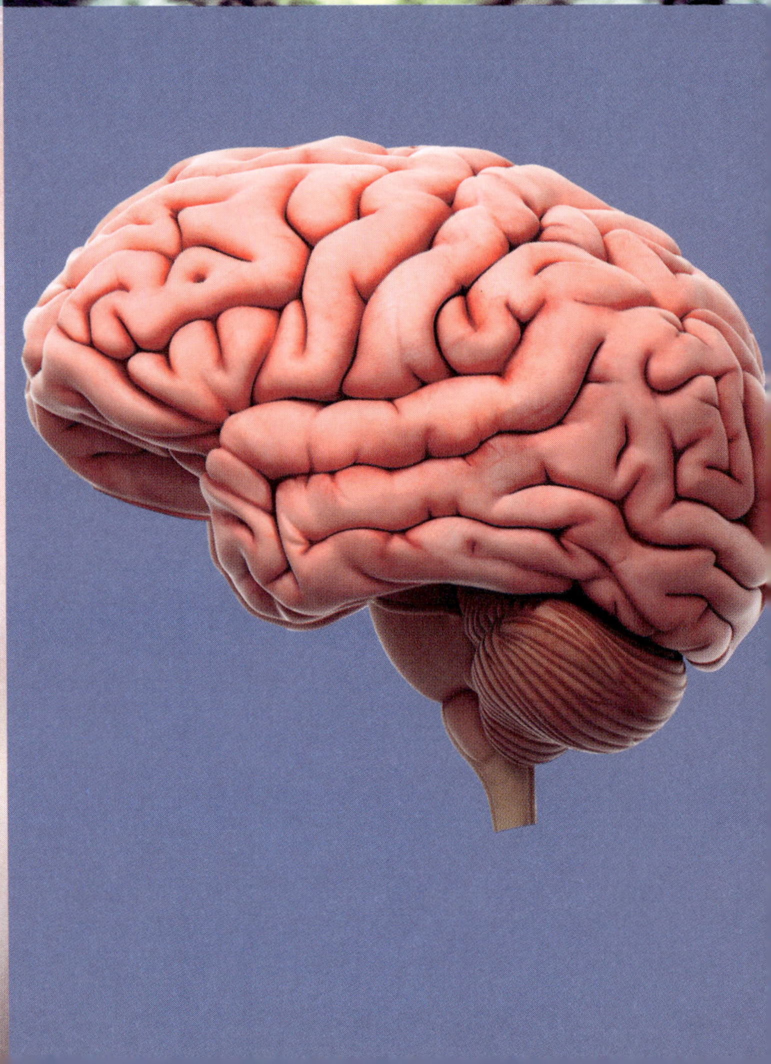

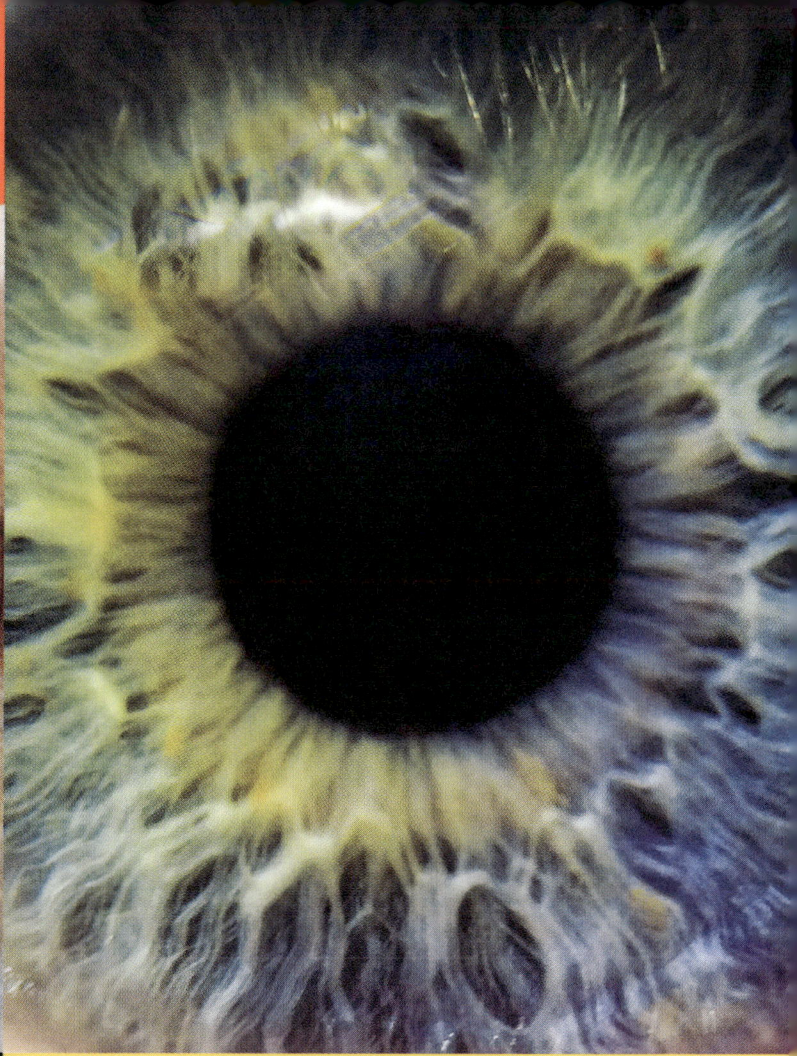

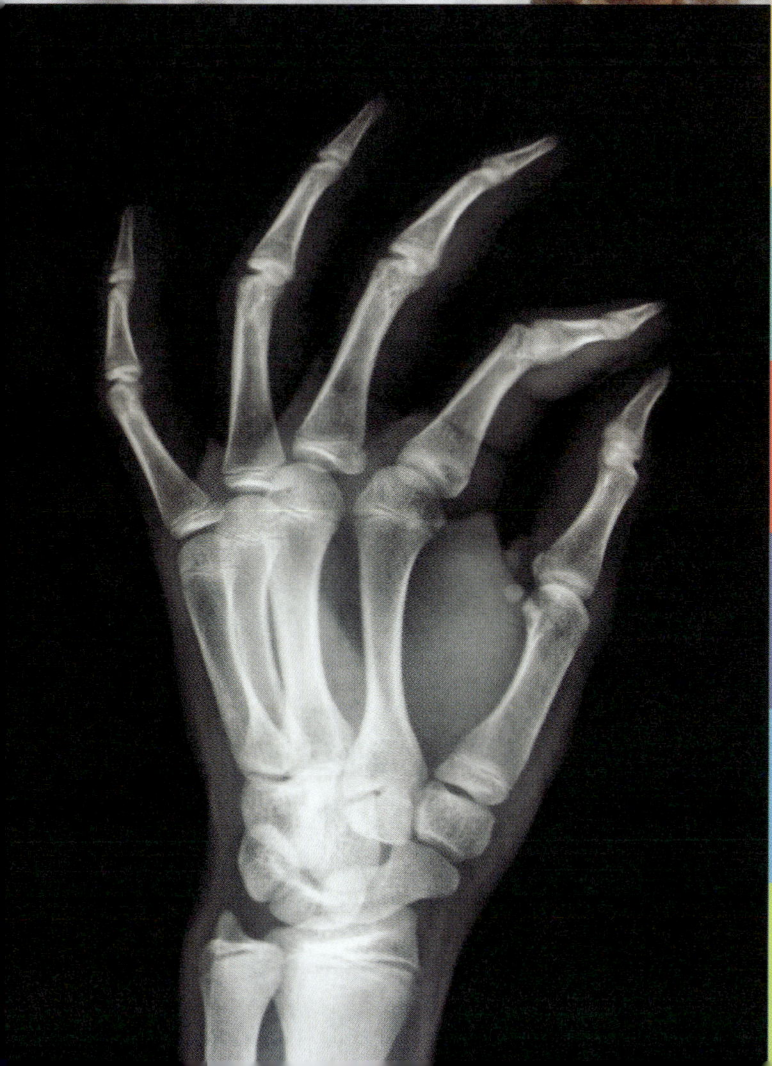

Twisty tongue

Long fingernails

Scan of a baby in its mother's belly

Model of the human brain

X-ray of a human hand

Human eye

FOOD

Why do cakes puff up in the oven? And other curious questions about things we eat

Why does fruit have seeds?

Fruits come in beautiful colours and shapes – and they taste delicious, too. Many plants grow their seeds inside eye-catching fruits in order to attract animals to eat them. When a bird or other animal eats the fruit, the seeds pass through its body. As the animal moves from place to place, it spreads seeds through its droppings – or poo. This helps new fruit plants grow far and wide.

WACKY FACT

There are peaches shaped a bit like doughnuts.

Some pomegranates contain more than 1,000 seeds.

Watermelons have the perfect name. Why?

Because they are made mostly of water!

Chimpanzees adore honey. They will climb tall trees to reach beehives.

Why do I like sweet things?

WACKY FACT

Most of your taste buds are on your tongue, but you also have taste buds on the roof of your mouth and in the back of your throat.

Most people love sweet things. So do lots of other animals. That's because before humans even existed, the only sweets around were natural ones like ripe fruit and honey. Sweetness was a sign of a good, nutritious meal. Nowadays humans make sweets that don't have much nutrition at all, but our sweet tooth still makes us want them.

Why does old food get mouldy?

If you forget about some leftovers in your fridge for a long time, or leave some bread in its packet for ages – uh-oh – you might find your food is covered in fuzzy stuff. That's mould. Mould comes from tiny particles called spores that float around in the air. When they land on food, they grow. They feed on your leftovers and get bigger.

WHO KNOWS?

A single spoonful of soil can contain thousands of different moulds. Scientists still haven't discovered most of the moulds that are out there.

If you look at mould under a microscope, it can look like tiny trees.

Mould may be yucky to find on your loaf of bread, but in nature, mould helps the planet. It breaks down all sorts of things, including food waste and dead plants.

Chocolate is the most popular sweet treat in the world.

Why does chocolate melt?

Everything melts, if it gets hot enough! When something melts, it turns from a solid to a liquid. Chocolate melts at about 31 degrees Celsius. Your body is warmer than that, so holding chocolate in your hand, or putting it in your mouth, warms it enough to melt it.

WACKY FACT

Chocolate comes from the seeds of the cacao tree. It takes about 40 seeds to make one bar of chocolate.

Why does chopping onions make me cry?

Chopping onions makes you cry because the onions are using self-defense. When any vegetable is damaged – by the teeth of a hungry animal or the knife of a hungry human – its cells are torn open. Many plants contain bitter-tasting substances to try to discourage creatures from eating them. Onions go even further. They give off a substance that gets in our eyes and makes them sting and water.

The biggest onion ever grown was heavier than a bowling ball.

WACKY FACT

Wearing goggles can help stop you from crying onion-tears. Goggles prevent onion fumes from getting into your eyes.

WHO KNOWS?

Scientists don't yet know why some people love stinky cheeses, while others find their odour disgusting.

Why are some cheeses stinky?

Pee-yew! Some cheeses smell like dirty socks. That's because cheesemakers grow special bacteria on the outsides of many cheeses. Bacteria are tiny living things made up of only one cell. These bacteria break down the outer layer of the cheese and release smelly gases. But that's not all. The bacteria also help give each kind of cheese its flavour.

Some of the gases that certain bacteria release when breaking down cheese are the same ones that make your feet smell!

Why are chillies spicy?

Your eyes are watering, your nose is running, you're sweating and your mouth feels like it's on fire. You must be eating chillies! Some chillies can make your mouth feel scorching hot. This is because of a substance called capsaicin. Capsaicin switches on the areas of your tongue and skin that normally sense heat. Then an alert goes to your brain and tricks it into thinking these areas are burning.

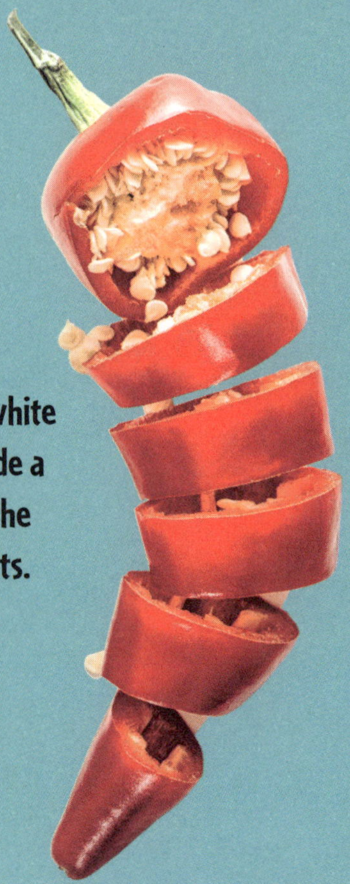

The soft white parts inside a chilli are the hottest bits.

Scotch bonnets look like tam-o'-shanter hats, which are popular in Scotland. That's how these chillies got their name.

According to Guinness World Records, the hottest chilli is the Carolina Reaper.

WACKY FACT

Birds can't taste chilli spice. Parrots can gobble the spicy flesh and seeds from the hottest types of chilli – no sweat!

Why does popcorn pop?

Popcorn starts as a hard kernel and ends up as a fluffy puffball.

Inside each kernel of popcorn is a tiny bit of water surrounded by a hard shell called a hull. If the kernel is heated to a high enough temperature, the water will turn into steam. With nowhere to go, the steam builds up pressure until the hull bursts. Then – POP! – the kernel explodes, releasing its fluffy inner parts.

WACKY FACT

Animals called binturongs smell like hot buttered popcorn. They live in forests in parts of Asia.

Why do beetroots grow underground?

We eat different parts of different plants. When we eat the lettuce plant, we munch the leaves. But beetroots, along with carrots and radishes, are the roots of the plant. Roots hold a plant firmly in the ground, allowing it to grow upwards towards the sun. Roots also absorb water and nutrients from the soil and carry them to the rest of the plant.

Beetroots come in all different colours, including red, purple, orange and yellow. Candy cane beetroots have red and white stripes.

WACKY FACT

If you eat beetroots, it can make your wee turn pink!

Each ingredient in a cake has a job. This is why it's important to follow a recipe exactly.

Why do cakes puff up in the oven?

When you beat butter, sugar, egg and flour together to make a cake, you trap tiny bubbles of air in the cake batter. Adding baking powder to cake batter creates even more bubbles. When you put the cake in the oven, the heat makes the bubbles grow bigger. This is what makes the cake rise.

When you cut a cake, you can see the bubbles of trapped air inside.

WACKY FACT

The tallest cake in the world was baked in Jakarta, Indonesia, in 2008. It was about as tall as a blue whale standing on its tail.

Why does ice cream sometimes give me a headache?

When you eat ice cream, it can sometimes be painful. When something cold touches the roof of your mouth or the back of your throat, blood vessels there tighten. Then, when warm air hits them, they widen again. These quick changes tell the brain that something painful is happening. When the brain gets these signals, the pain is felt in the forehead.

Scientists call an ice cream headache 'sphenopalatine ganglioneuralgia' (sfeen-oh-pal-a-tine gang-glee-oh-nyoo-rall-juh).

WHO KNOWS?

Experts don't agree about how to stop an ice cream headache. But pressing your tongue to the roof of your mouth might help.

WACKY FACT

André Ortolf of Germany holds the world record for most jelly eaten with chopsticks in one minute.

Wibble Wobble

Why does jelly wobble?

The key ingredients in jelly are gelatin and water. Gelatin is made up of tiny particles that cling tightly together in a spiral. When you add hot water, they come apart. When you pop the jelly in the refrigerator, the tiny particles try to link together again. They form a web that stretches from one side of the jelly to the other. Water gets trapped in the web's spaces, giving the jelly its wobble.

Jelly can be moulded into any shape.

Why do bananas turn brown?

Bananas give off a gas that makes them ripen. This gas turns bananas from a deep green to a delicious yellow. If you don't eat a ripe banana quickly, the gas will make the banana turn brown and squishy.

Green: it's not quite ready yet. Unripe bananas contain chlorophyll, which gives plants their greenish colour.

Yellow: perfect for eating. A ripe banana has a yellow peel and is soft inside.

Brown: Don't throw it away! Overripe bananas are perfect for making banana bread.

Putting bananas in a paper bag traps their gases and makes the bananas ripen faster.

WACKY FACT

Some bananas have blue skin instead of yellow.

A bunch of bananas is called a hand.

WACKY FACT

The first raisin crop in California, U.S.A., was an accident! The grapes were left on the vine for too long. They shrivelled up but turned out to be delicious.

Why are raisins wrinkly?

Raisins are made by putting grapes out in the sun. As the sun's heat warms the grapes, the water inside them leaves the fruit and enters the air. As the grapes slowly dry out over time, they get smaller and darker. Their skins shrivel and wrinkle. The grapes have become raisins!

It takes about two to three weeks for grapes to turn into raisins when they are dried in the sun.

Wow! What's that?

Here are some extraordinary foods. Can you match each one to its name?

Answers on page 271

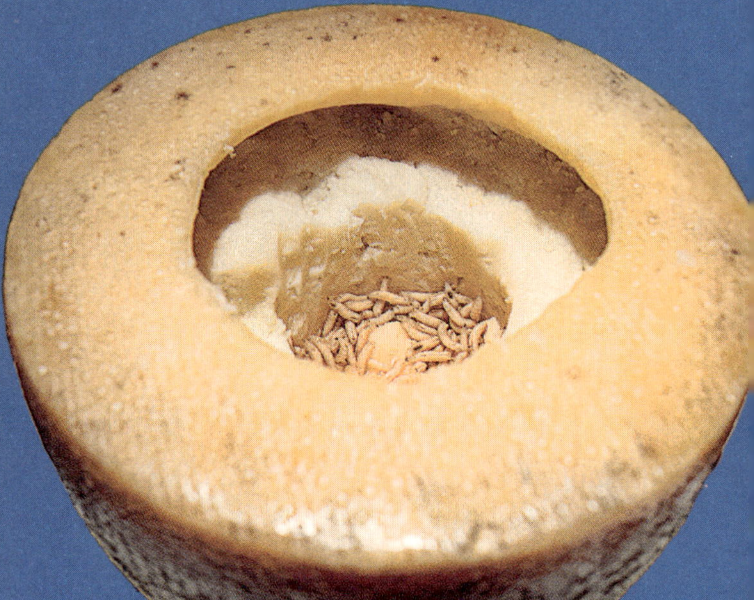

Whisked egg whites

Casu marzu maggot-infested cheese

Dragon fruit

Glow-in-the-dark ice cream

Romanesco broccoli

Blue bananas

HOW STUFF WORKS

Why do trains run on tracks? And other curious questions about machines and inventions

554

Why are rockets pointy?

When a rocket shoots up into the sky, its front end hits the air. The air pushes back against the rocket, and this slows it down. A rocket with a flat nose would hit the air head-on. A rocket with a pointed nose hits the air at an angle. This lessens the slowing force of the air and helps the rocket fly far and fast. Whoosh!

WACKY FACT

The first rockets were invented in China. They were used to launch fireworks!

A rocket headed to space travels almost 80 times faster than the world's fastest car.

A helicopter can fly sideways and backwards.

WACKY FACT

Some helicopters are used to fight fires. They dump buckets filled with lots of water on flames from above.

Why are helicopters so loud?

WHOP, WHOP, WHOP! It's the noise of a helicopter overhead. A helicopter lifts off the ground using its rotor, or spinning blades. As the helicopter flies, each blade creates a bunch of whirling air, known as a vortex, at its tip. As the next blade hits the vortex, it makes a loud sound.

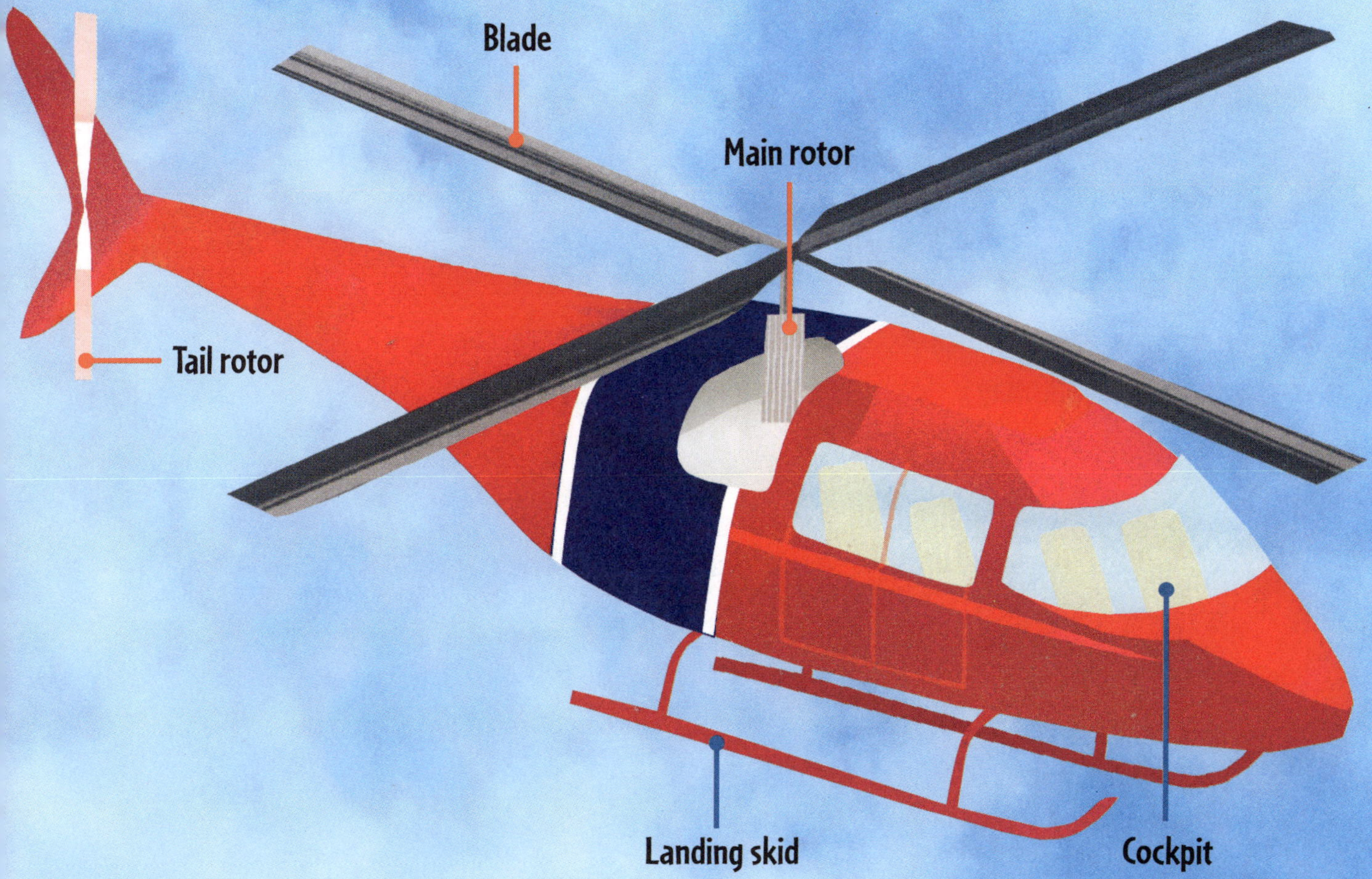

Why do cars have horns?

When cars were first invented, there were no traffic lights. Roads were full of people and carts pulled by horses. At first, drivers used whistles and bells to warn others to clear the road. Later, they switched to horns. They honked the horns by squeezing an air-filled bulb, similar to a bike horn. Today, horns are powered by electricity. But the honk still means 'Watch out!'

One early horn like this one was advertised with the slogan, 'You press as you steer and your pathway is clear'.

WACKY FACT

Race cars don't have horns.

AOOGHA!
358
ANNIE

WACKY FACT

Train wheels are designed in a special shape, which is wider on the inside than the outside. This shape allows them to roll along a curved track without veering off one way or the other.

Why do trains run on tracks?

Tracks allow trains to transport much heavier things than cars or lorries on a road ever could. When a locomotive engine pulls along the carriages behind it, the train's steel wheels run easily over the smooth steel track. Passenger trains carry hundreds of people. Freight trains carry everything from cement and tractors to cheese and fruit.

Trains have to follow the direction of the tracks, so they don't need steering wheels.

Why do buildings have lifts?

In the 1800s, engineers used metal beams to build the first skyscrapers, which were up to 20 storeys tall. Imagine having to climb stairs to the top floor! That's why lifts were invented. A lift car has thick cables attached to its top. These cables go up the shaft and around a wheel at the top. The cables are attached to a weight on the other end that balances the car, making it easier for the car to move smoothly. A motor turns the wheel to move the lift car up and down.

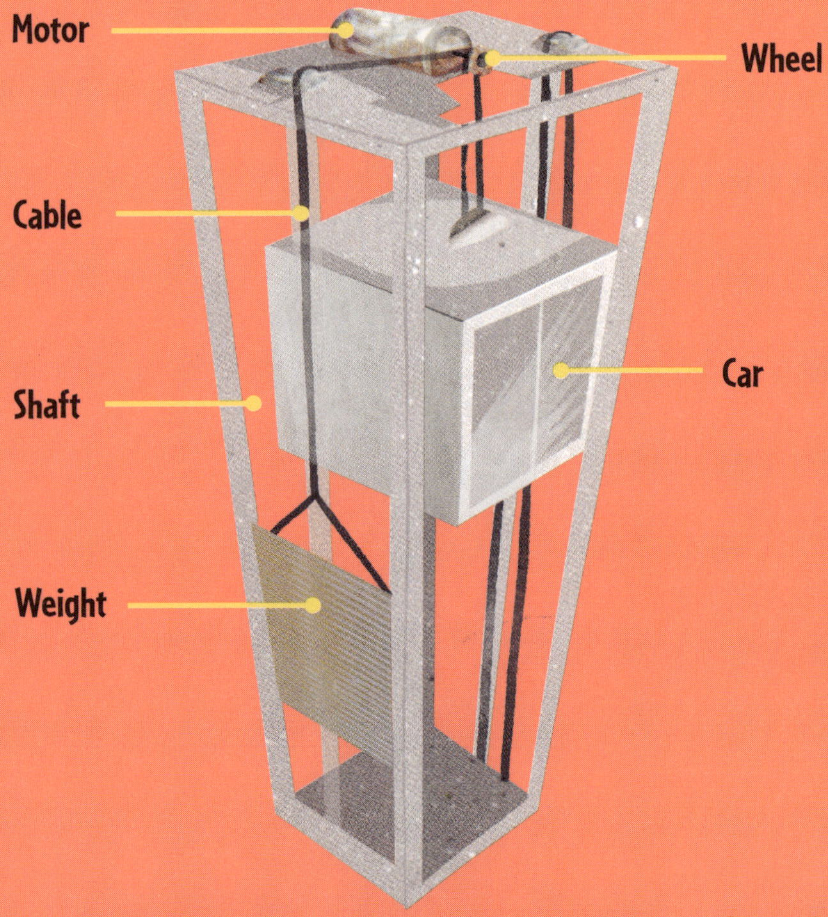

WACKY FACT

Scientists are working on the first-ever space lift. They hope to one day take people and supplies from Earth to space with the push of a button!

Mirrors reverse images. So your right hand in real life looks as though it's your left hand in the reflection.

Why can I see myself in a mirror?

WACKY FACT

Babies don't recognise themselves in a mirror until they are about 18 months old.

Mirrors help you brush your hair and spot that piece of lettuce stuck in your teeth. But how do they work? A mirror is made up of a piece of glass backed by a thin layer of metal. This metal is ultra-smooth – so smooth that all light that hits it bounces back in exactly the same direction it came from. Your eyes see this bounced-back light as your reflection.

Any super-smooth surface can be reflective. That's why you can see yourself in the still water of a lake, pond or puddle.

Why don't skyscrapers fall over?

Skyscrapers sway in the wind. If you stood at the top of the 163-floor Burj Khalifa in Dubai, United Arab Emirates, you'd feel the building moving 2 metres back and forth! But these buildings don't topple because their foundations, or bases, extend far underground, like the roots of a tree. They are also built of concrete strengthened with steel rods and beams.

WACKY FACT

Termite mounds are nature's skyscrapers. They can be more than 9 metres tall. Holes and tunnels allow air to flow through, keeping the mound cool. Human architects have copied this design.

WACKY FACT

Sometimes, rubbish can be riches! In 2018, seven gold bars worth £240,000 were found in a bin at an airport in South Korea.

Why does a bin lorry crush the rubbish?

Crushing rubbish helps bin lorries fit as much as possible inside. Once the rubbish is dropped in, a large metal blade comes down to crush it. Scrunch! When the lorry is full, the driver heads to a landfill. There, the rubbish is dumped. But not all our rubbish is simply thrown away. In lots of places, recycling vans go to neighbourhoods and pick up materials such as glass, paper and plastic.

Why do batteries run out?

Batteries have two ends, a positive end and a negative end. The stuff inside the battery at the negative end gives off lots of particles called electrons. The stuff inside the battery at the positive end makes particles that attract electrons. When you connect a wire between the two ends, the electrons flow from the negative end to the positive end. Flowing electrons are called electrical current. When you connect something like a games console or a torch to the wire between the two ends of the battery, the electrical current powers the gadget. When the stuff inside the battery can't give off any more electrons, the battery dies.

WHO KNOWS?

The world's longest-lasting battery has been in use for more than 175 years! Located in Oxfordshire, England, the battery powers two small bells. Scientists aren't sure how it's still working.

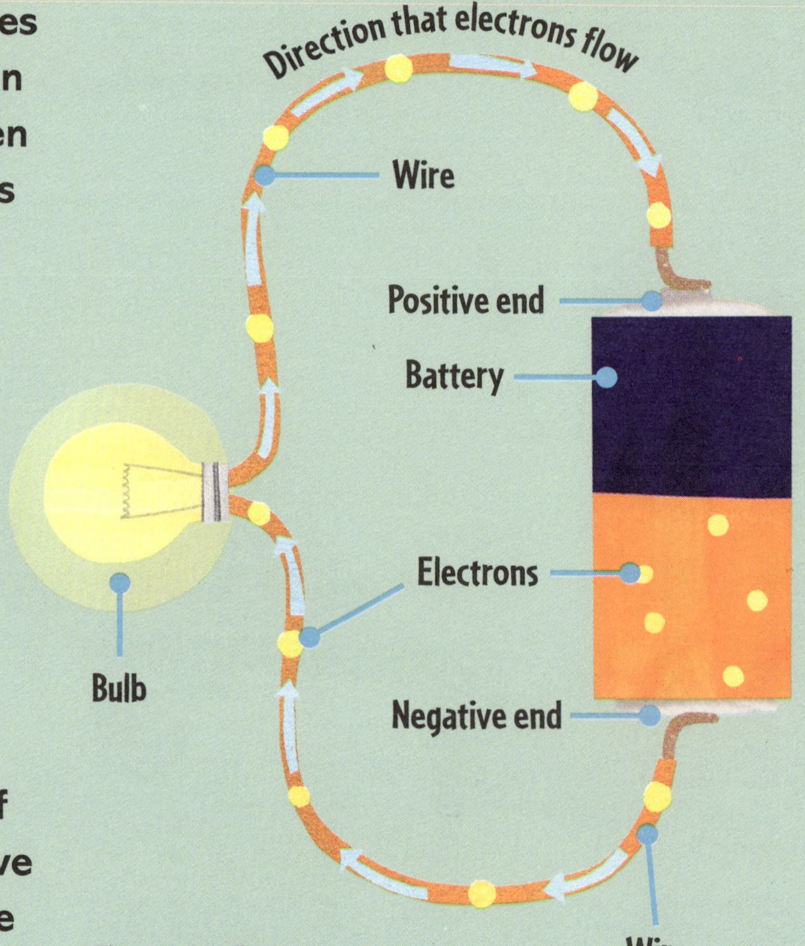

Electricity flows in a loop called a circuit.

The first battery-powered torches lasted only a few seconds. Today, torches can last hours on just a couple of batteries, making them perfect for helping you read a good book under the covers.

The trails behind planes are made of water, not smog or smoke.

Why do aeroplanes make trails in the sky?

Walk outside on a cold winter day and you will see your breath in the air. This happens for the same reason aeroplanes leave white trails, called contrails, in their paths. Jet engines create hot, humid air. When the hot air hits the cold air high in the sky, the water inside the air changes from a gas into tiny ice crystals. This makes a white cloud.

WACKY FACT

Sometimes aeroplanes create contrails that appear rainbow-coloured. This happens when the sun shines through the ice crystals of the contrail at just the right angle.

Why do we flush the toilet?

Press down on the flush and your waste goes whirling away. We flush toilets to get rid of our poo and wee, which keeps germs away and stops our homes from getting smelly. Most toilets flush waste down a pipe called a sewer, where it meets up with other household wastes, like soapy water from the shower. These wastes, called sewage, flow into a sewage treatment plant that removes the waste from the water. Then, the clean water is pumped into a local lake, a river or the ocean.

WACKY FACT

Some sewage pipes are so big that a bus could fit inside!

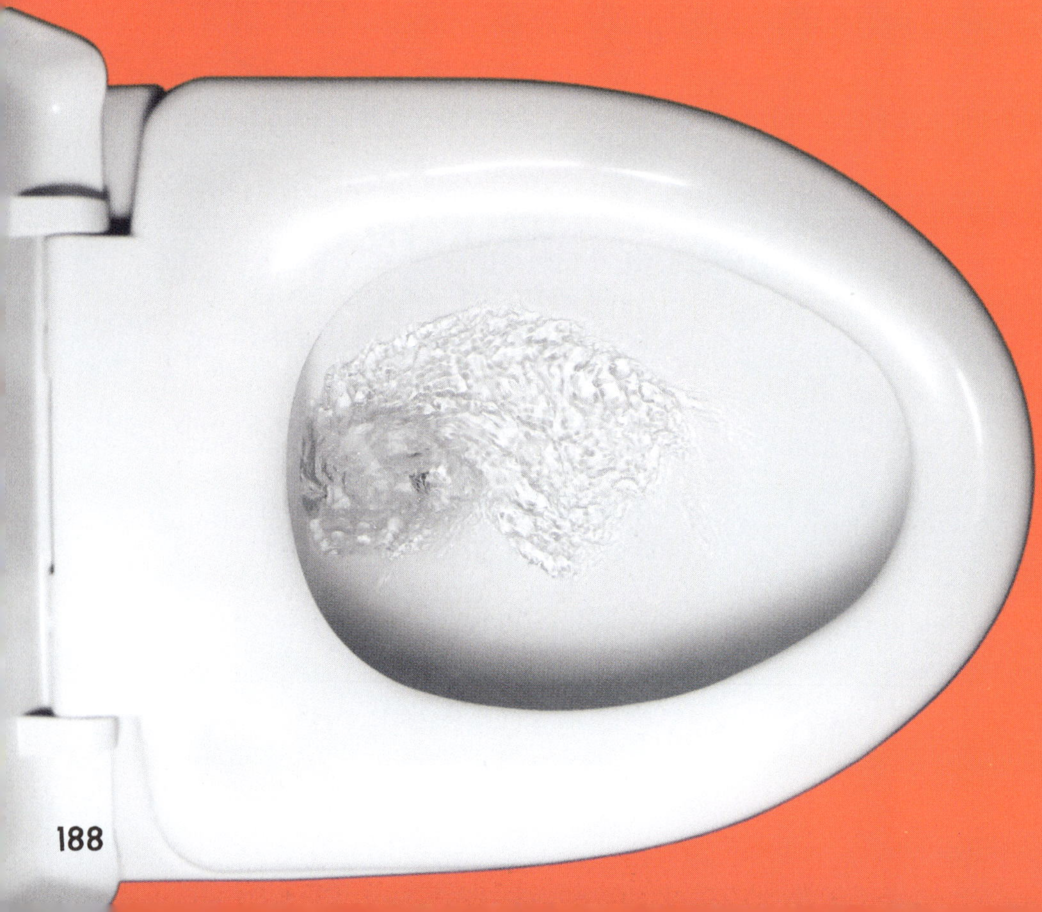

Not all toilet water goes into a sewer. Some homes have septic tanks. These underground tanks act as much smaller versions of sewage treatment plants.

Pipes carry away dirty water from our toilets, as well as from our washing machines, baths and sinks.

The dirty water is flushed away to a septic tank or into sewer pipes.

The first rubber ducks didn't float. They were chew toys!

Why does my rubber duck float?

Some objects, such as a stone, sink. Others, such as a rubber duck, float. The difference is in their buoyancy. When an object is placed in water, its weight pushes some of the water away. If the object weighs more than the water that it pushes away, it sinks. Because a rubber duck is hollow inside, it weighs less than the water it pushes away. This makes it float.

WACKY FACT

In 1992, a container from a ship fell overboard and its contents – 28,000 rubber ducks! – spilled into the ocean. Some of them are still floating in the sea today.

Why do we have traffic lights?

WACKY FACT

The first traffic lights had only red and green signals. Yellow was added later.

When the first cars hit the road, there were no traffic lights. But as more and more vehicles sped off, cities began installing traffic lights to help prevent accidents. At first, people directed traffic by standing in booths at the top of towers, blowing whistles and shining red and green lights to signal drivers. Today, traffic lights are powered by electricity.

In 1918, the first traffic towers were installed in New York City. They were 7 metres high and made of bronze.

When the green light shines, it means GO!
A yellow light means 'stop if it's safe to do so'.
When the red light shines, it means STOP.

WHO KNOWS?

Scientists don't fully understand why ice is so slippery. Ice is covered with a thin layer of water, but experts are still investigating where this layer comes from and how it works.

Why do ice skates have blades?

The blade on an ice skate does two main jobs. When it's pointed forwards, its thin, smooth surface allows the skater to glide quickly and easily along. When positioned at an angle, it digs into the ice so the skater can push forwards or stop.

Figure skates have saw-like ridges at the front to help skaters perform tricks like jumps and spins.

Wow! What's that?

Here are some crazy creations.
Can you match each one to its name?

Answers on page 271

Bubble car

Funhouse mirror

Underwater scooter

Outdoor lift

Twisting skyscraper

Gold-plated toilet

EARTH

Why are flowers colourful? And other curious questions about our planet

Why do earthquakes happen?

The surface of Earth is made up of giant plates of rock that fit together like a jigsaw puzzle. These plates are always in motion, but they move very, very slowly. Their edges are rough, and sometimes, two plates will snag on each other. When the pressure builds up enough, the plates will suddenly jerk free. This makes the ground shake.

WHO KNOWS?

Scientists can't predict exactly when earthquakes will happen.

There are seven major plates. The area where two plates meet is called a fault.

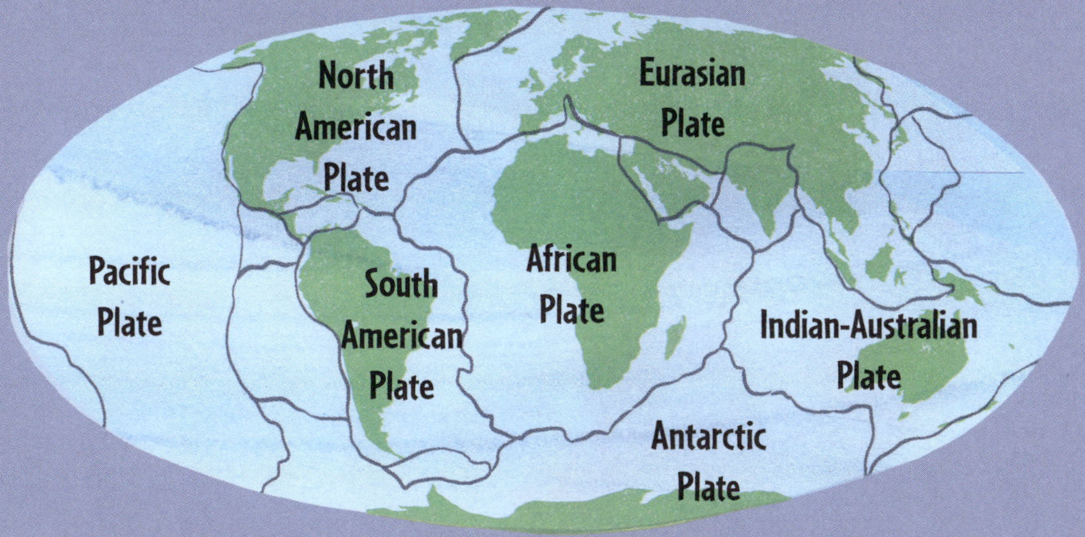

Earthquakes can topple buildings and buckle roads.

Volcanoes are found on land, on the ocean floor and even under ice caps.

Why do volcanoes erupt?

Deep under Earth's surface, it's so hot that rock melts. This melted rock is called magma. Magma is lighter than the solid rock around it, so it rises. It pushes its way up and out through cracks (called vents) to reach Earth's surface. Then, it's called lava. Sometimes, lava flows out slowly. Other times, it shoots straight up into the air!

WACKY FACT

Lava can be about 1,200 degrees Celsius. That's hot enough to melt gold.

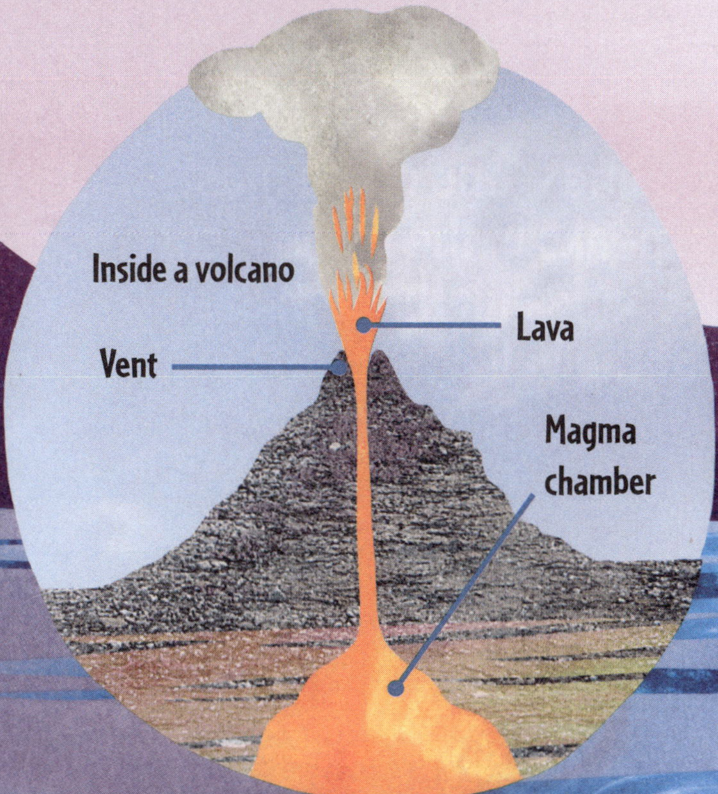

Why does the ocean have waves?

The waves you usually see at the beach are created by wind. Wind blowing over the ocean creates little ripples on the surface. The more the wind blows, the bigger the waves grow. Waves travel in a straight line until something gets in their way – like a beach. Scientists have tracked waves as they travelled across the ocean for more than a week!

WHO KNOWS?

Sometimes enormous waves called rogue waves appear out of nowhere in the open ocean. They can top 30 metres. Scientists don't yet agree on the main cause of these mega waves.

Dolphins sometimes ride waves, just like human surfers do.

The peak of a wave is called the crest. The lowest point is called the trough.

WACKY FACT

Not all dinosaurs died out. Birds are a kind of dinosaur that survived the extinction and still live on Earth today.

T. rex was a meat-eating dinosaur with large teeth and a bite strong enough to crush the bones of its prey.

Why can't I meet a *T. rex*?

All of the tyrannosaurs died out long before there were any humans on the planet. Dinosaurs were once the most powerful creatures on Earth. But that changed 66 million years ago, when a giant space rock slammed into the ocean off the coast of Mexico. This caused violent earthquakes and raging fires, and soot and dust choked the sky. About three-quarters of living things were wiped out.

Even though almost all dinosaurs died, fossils like this one of a *T. rex* give us clues about how dinosaurs looked and behaved when they were alive.

Why are flowers colourful?

Most plant parts are green. But flowers can have brilliant colours. Their colours get the attention of creatures such as bees and birds. These pollinators carry pollen from one plant to another, so plants can make seeds to make more plants. Many birds prefer red flowers, while bees like blue, white or purple flowers.

WACKY FACT

Many flowers have patterns that humans can't see, but bees can. The patterns direct bees where to land on a flower, like the lights on an aeroplane runway.

Red, tube-shaped flowers appeal to hummingbirds.

WACKY FACT

Rainbows are actually circles, but we can only see part of them from the ground.

Why do rainbows appear after a rainstorm?

A rainbow appears when sunlight shines on a floating drop of water. It may not look like it, but sunlight is made up of all different colours. The light enters the water droplet and bounces back out. Each colour bounces back at a slightly different angle. As the light travels, its colours separate. When the light reaches your eyes, you see the colours of the rainbow.

Why is the sky blue?

Sunlight is made up of the colours of the rainbow – red, orange, yellow, green, blue, indigo, violet and all the colours in between. All light travels in waves. Red light travels in long, lazy waves. Blue light travels in the shortest waves. When sunlight hits gas and dust in the air, its light waves bounce around all over the sky before bouncing into our eyes. The waves that bounce around the most are the short blue light waves. So, we see the colour blue coming from the whole sky.

WACKY FACT

If you drove up through the sky at about the speed a car drives on the motorway, it would take about one hour to get to space.

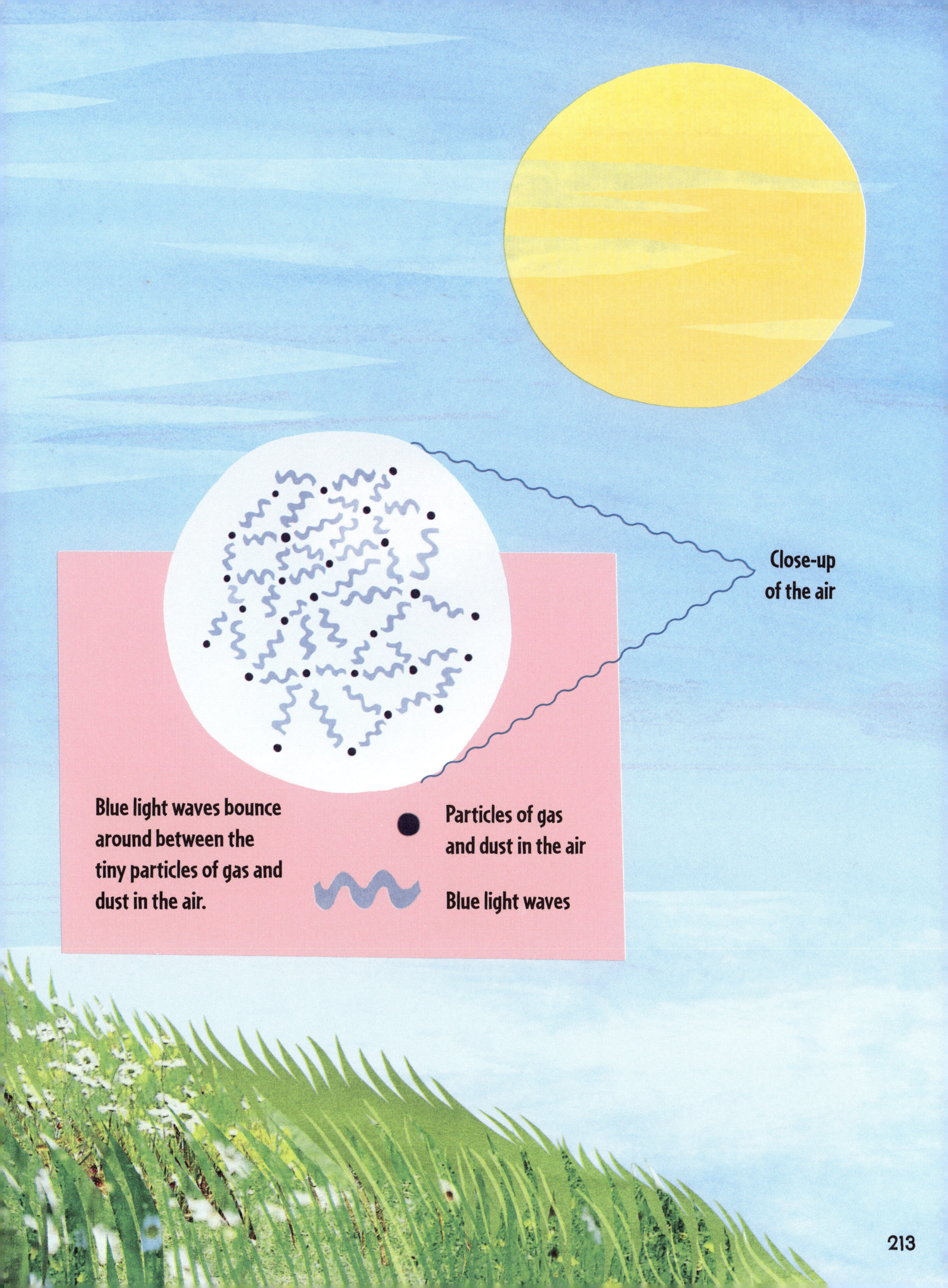
Close-up
of the air
Blue light waves bounce
around between the
tiny particles of gas and
dust in the air.
Particles of gas
and dust in the air
Blue light waves

WACKY FACT

There's a very good chance the water you drink is the same water a thirsty dinosaur gulped down millions of years ago. That's because the same water has been cycling on Earth since our planet formed.

Why does it rain?

Clouds are made of tiny drops of water. Those water droplets bounce around and bump into each other, forming bigger droplets. Eventually, they become too heavy to float in the sky, and they fall from the clouds as rain. This is a step in the water cycle, which moves water around the planet.

1 Heat from the sun warms water in the ocean, lakes and rivers, turning it into a gas called water vapour that rises into the sky.

2 When the water vapour gets high enough, it cools, turns back into water droplets and forms clouds.

Why are mountains so tall?

When the giant plates of rock that make up Earth's surface smash together, their edges crumple like a squashed tin can and push huge slabs of rock upwards. This is one way mountains form. The plates underneath India and Asia began colliding more than 25 million years ago. Mount Everest is one of the mountains that formed there. The plates are still colliding, and Mount Everest is still growing today.

WHO KNOWS?

The Gamburtsev Mountains, also known as the 'ghost mountains', are buried deep beneath the ice and snow in Antarctica. Scientists don't yet know for certain how and when they formed.

Mountains can also form when lava from a constantly erupting volcano cools and hardens, layer upon layer. That's how Mauna Kea in Hawaii formed. It started all the way at the bottom of the ocean and is now the tallest mountain in the world measured from bottom to top.

Mount Everest is the world's highest mountain above sea level, at 8,849 metres.

WHO KNOWS?

Scientists don't yet know why some types of sand are softer than others. The way sand works is still a bit of a mystery.

The sand on each beach in the world is as unique as a fingerprint.

Why are beaches sandy or pebbly?

Walk across a beach and you're stepping on material that took millions of years to form. Rocks bounce down rivers and streams, breaking into smaller pieces as they go. When they reach the beach, waves break them down even more. The sizes of the rock pieces come from the energy of the waves: calm waves in bays make fine sand while powerful waves that slam against cliffs make pebbles.

Pebbles become smooth over time as water flows over pieces of rock again and again.

Why do leaves fall off some trees?

Leaves turn sunlight into food for trees. To do this, they need water, which travels all the way from the soil up the trunk to the leaves. In the winter, water can freeze, damaging the leaves, so lots of trees drop their leaves when cold weather starts. During the winter, these trees rest.

WACKY FACT

Trees can communicate with each other. They do it through a huge, living underground network that is connected to their roots. It is sometimes called the Wood Wide Web.

Hedgehogs build cosy nests made of dead leaves, twigs and feathers in which they can snooze the winter away.

As autumn begins, the green leaves turn red, orange and yellow.

WACKY FACT

Geodes can also form when animals burrow in the ground. Later, this soil hardens into rock with a hollow space inside, where crystals then grow.

The Pulpí Geode in Spain contains human-sized crystals!

Why do some rocks have crystals inside?

Some rocks have empty spaces inside. One reason for this is that an air bubble can get trapped in lava as it cools into rock. Over time, minerals in water seep through the rock into the hollow space. The minerals cling to the insides of the rock, forming tiny crystals. When this happens over and over again for millions of years, the crystals grow. These crystal-filled rocks are known as geodes.

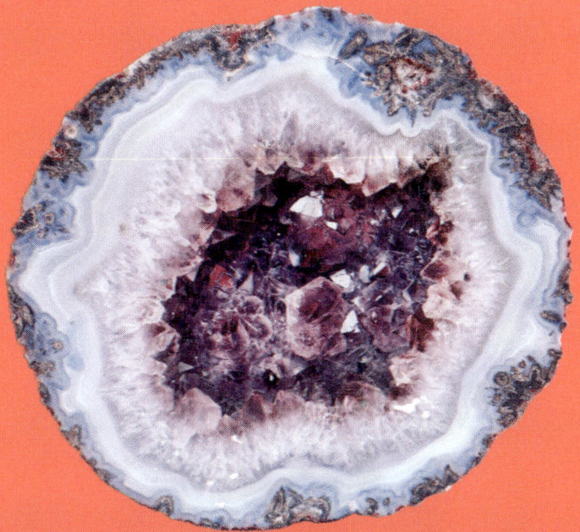

This geode contains a type of crystal called amethyst.

Why are clouds different shapes?

Clouds might look like fluffy cotton. But they're actually made of millions of water droplets or ice crystals so tiny and lightweight that they float. Different air temperatures can make clouds look thin and wispy or so thick they cover the sky. Wind stretches and squishes clouds, changing their shapes.

Cirrus clouds have a wispy shape.

Stratus clouds are long and flat.

Cumulus clouds are white and puffy.

WHO KNOWS?

Water droplets and ice crystals need to cluster around tiny particles in the air in order to form clouds. Experts know what some of these particles are, such as dust. But others are a mystery.

Clouds sometimes look like other things! What do you see in this cloud?

People, plants and animals have adapted to living in deserts, including the Sahara, pictured here.

WACKY FACT

The saguaro cactus, which lives in the desert in the United States and Mexico, can live for 200 years.

Desert-dwelling fennec foxes use their large ears to listen for insects and other prey under the sand. Their ears also help release body heat to keep the foxes cool.

Why are deserts dry?

Deserts are areas of land that get very little snow or rain. In a desert, less than 25 centimetres of rain falls in a whole year. Deserts can be hot or cold. Antarctica is Earth's largest and driest desert, and it's freezing. The world's largest hot desert is the Sahara in Africa.

Wow! What's that?

Here are some wonders of nature.
Can you match each one to its name?

Answers on page 271

Clouds on Mount Fuji, Japan

Waterspout

Fossilised dinosaur footprint

Methuselah, the oldest tree in the world

Magnified snowflakes

Stalagmites and stalactites

SPACE

Why do astronauts wear suits? And other curious questions about the cosmos

X+
Z+

Why can we only see stars at night?

Look up on a clear night and you'll see nearly 5,000 stars. But in the daytime they seem to disappear. They are still there, it's just that we can't see them anymore. Stars are faraway balls of burning gas, and their light travels trillions of miles through space. But when the sun, the closest star to our planet, lights up the sky during the day, it is too bright for us to see those more distant stars.

Stars are born in giant clouds of gas and dust called nebulae.

WHO KNOWS?

Scientists think it's likely that nearly every star has at least one planet orbiting it, the way our Earth goes around the sun. They are still trying to figure out how many planets there are in the universe.

Why do stars twinkle?

Stars don't actually twinkle, they shine with steady light. Stars just appear to twinkle when we see them from the surface of Earth. A star's light travels through space and reaches our atmosphere, the blanket of gas that surrounds our planet. Moving air in the atmosphere bends the light from the stars, bouncing some of it away from us and some of it towards us. That makes the star look like it's twinkling.

WACKY FACT

Stars are different colours. The hottest ones are blue.

Blue and red stars glow brightly in this picture taken by the Hubble Space Telescope.

Why is it dark in space?

Even though space is full of bright stars, it looks black. That's because light travels in a straight line unless something is in its path to bend it. On Earth, sunlight bounces around between dust and other particles as it passes through the atmosphere. That lights up the sky. But in space, there is no atmosphere to bounce light around. That makes space appear mostly dark.

The moon is Earth's closest neighbour in space. Here you can see the bumpy surface of the moon, where space rocks have slammed into its surface.

WHO KNOWS?

Space has a smell. Astronauts describe it as 'seared steak', 'hot metal', and 'burnt almond cookies'. Scientists don't yet know what makes the smell.

Space is completely silent.

WHO KNOWS?

The sun's atmosphere (or the blanket of gases around the sun) is hotter than the sun's surface. Scientists aren't sure why.

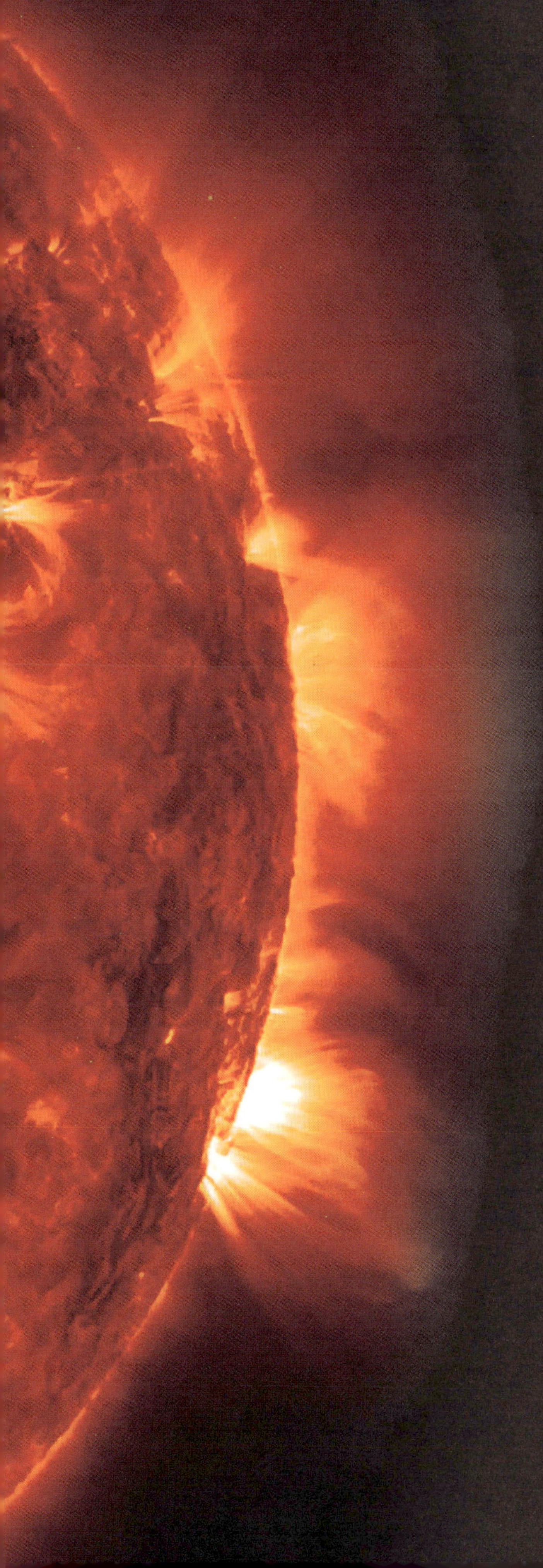

Why does the sun shine?

The sun looks small in our sky, but it's actually a massive ball of burning gas. Its size gives it tremendously strong gravity. That crushing gravity makes the pressure and temperature inside the sun extremely high, which causes the sun's gas – hydrogen – to turn into another gas – helium. This change creates heat and light.

The core is the centre of the sun. At 15 million degrees Celsius, this is the hottest part.

Why are planets round?

Planets get their shape from gravity. This pulling force makes rocks, gas and dust clump together in space. As more and more stuff sticks together, the gravity of the growing planet becomes stronger, pulling it into a rough ball.

WACKY FACT

Jupiter is thicker in the middle because it spins really fast. The spinning makes Jupiter bulge outwards, like pizza dough being spun in the air.

Mercury and Venus are the planets that are closest to being perfectly round.

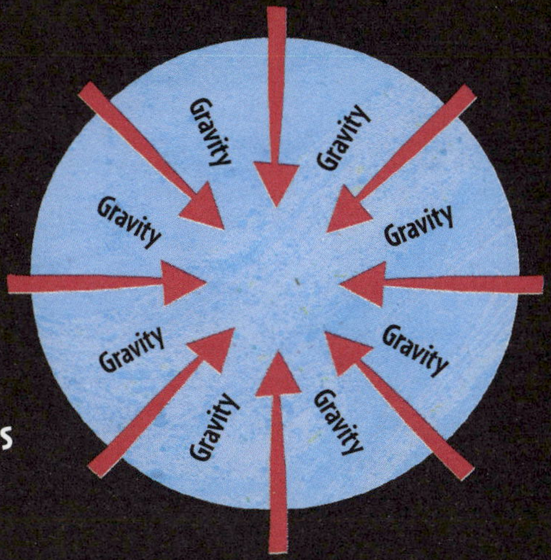

A planet's gravity pulls everything towards the centre of it. This makes it form a ball shape.

Why is Mars red?

Mars is visible in the night sky without a telescope.

The planet Mars is one of the brightest objects in the night sky. If you look closely you can even see its colour – red! This bright colour comes from rust, the same stuff you sometimes find on nails or old cars that have been left outside for a long time. Mars is covered with dust made mostly from iron, the same material those nails and cars are made of. Over millions of years, the iron dust has rusted, turning the planet red.

WACKY FACT

The sunsets on Mars are blue.

Why does Saturn have rings?

Saturn's rings aren't solid. They're made of billions of pieces of ice and rock. Scientists aren't sure, but some think the rings could have formed when icy and rocky objects got too close to Saturn and were shredded apart by Saturn's gravity. Some of these pieces are too small to see, while others are as big as a bus.

Saturn isn't the only planet with rings. Neptune, Jupiter and Uranus have them, too. They're just harder to see.

WHO KNOWS?

Saturn has seven main rings and many smaller rings – possibly up to 1,000! Experts aren't sure of the exact number.

Saturn's rings are so wide that if they surrounded Earth, they would stretch all the way to the moon!

Neptune was named for the Roman god of the sea.

WHO KNOWS?

Neptune is the windiest planet in the solar system, with winds of 1,770 kilometres per hour. Researchers aren't sure what causes these mega winds.

Why is Neptune blue?

Astronomers caught their first up close glimpse of Neptune in 1989, when NASA's *Voyager 2* spacecraft flew by. The photograph it snapped showed Neptune's ocean-like colour. But Neptune is not a water world. Instead, it's a giant ball of slushy ice surrounded by thick clouds. Those clouds contain a gas called methane. It is the methane that makes the planet blue.

Neptune is the most distant planet in the solar system.

Why do we have night and day?

As Earth moves around the sun, it also spins on an axis – an imaginary line that goes through its centre. As it spins, each side of Earth takes turns facing the sun. The sun's heat and light touch the side of Earth that faces it: we call this day. The other side of Earth is facing away from the sun. That makes it colder and darker: we call this night. Earth makes one full spin every 24 hours.

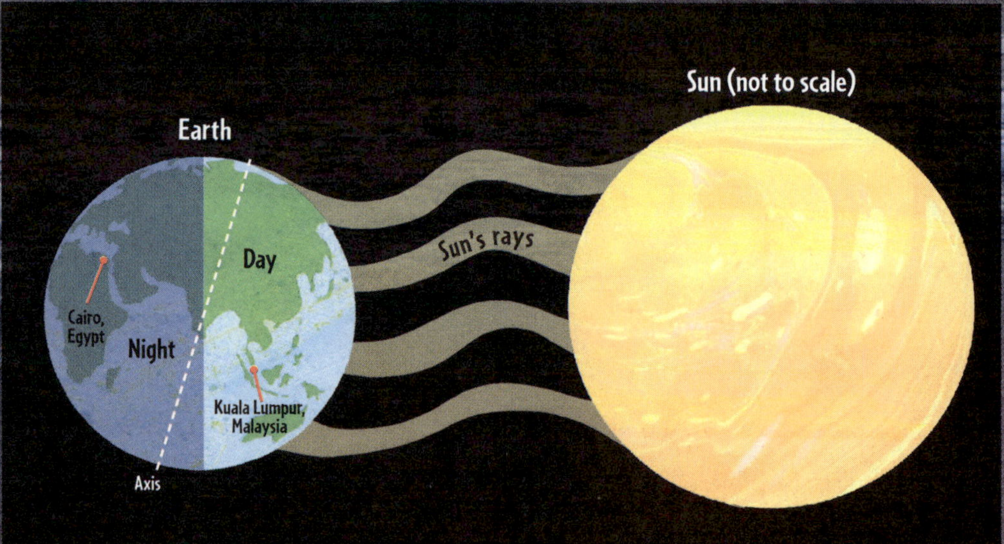

When it's night-time in Cairo, it's daytime in Kuala Lumpur.

The sun appears to move across the sky. But this is really because Earth is spinning.

WACKY FACT

Earth spins at a speed of about 1,700 kilometres per hour. That's about seven times faster than a race car!

WACKY FACT

Some planets in the solar system have several moons. Scientists have found 53 around Saturn. And they are still looking for more.

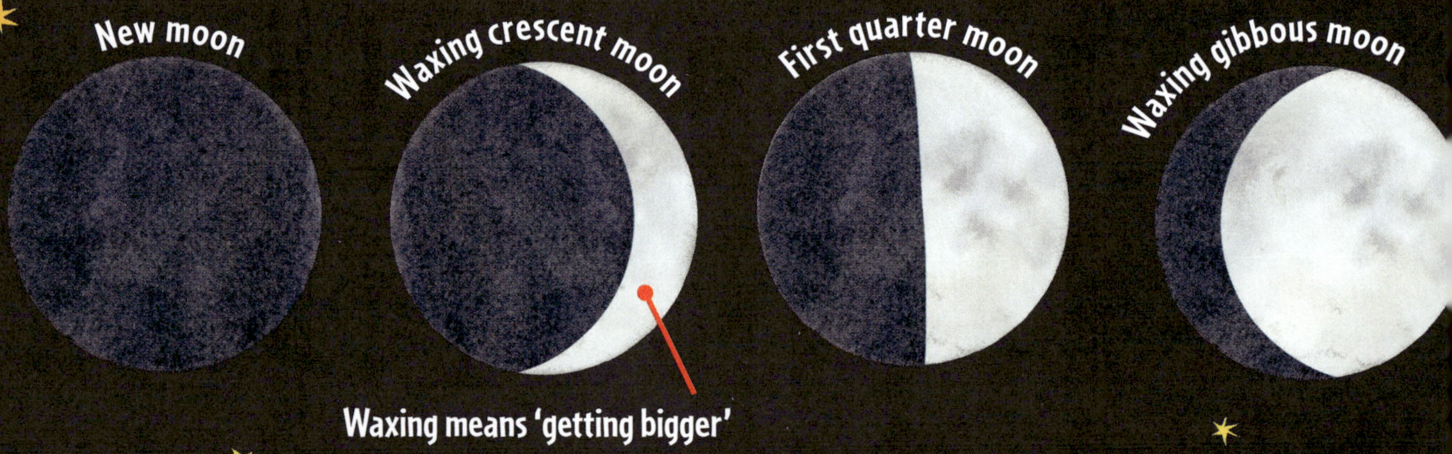

Why does the moon change shape?

The moon is always the same shape – round. But when we look at the moon from Earth, it seems to change day to day. That's because we can only see the part of the moon that is lit up by the sun. As the moon orbits Earth, the part we see changes. Sometimes we can only see a sliver. Other times, we can see the whole thing: a full moon!

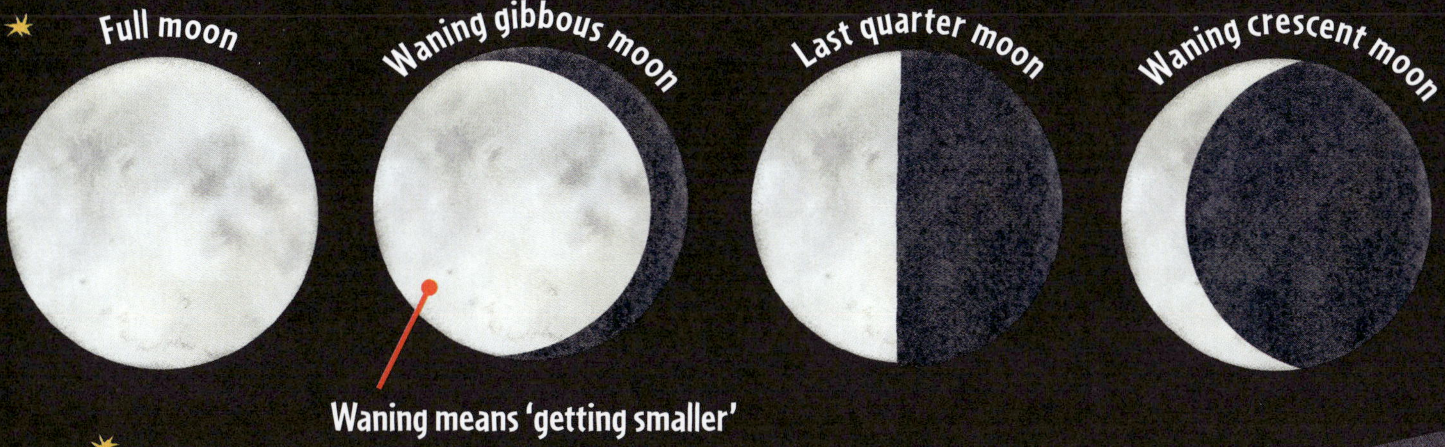

Why does an eclipse happen?

Eclipses happen because sometimes the sun, moon and Earth form a straight line, and Earth or the moon block the sun's light. An eclipse of the moon happens when Earth blocks sunlight from hitting the moon's surface. To us, it looks like the moon turns a coppery red colour. An eclipse of the sun happens when the moon blocks the sun's light from hitting Earth.

WACKY FACT

Birds such as hawks and doves often go to roost, or rest, during an eclipse of the sun. The darkness tricks them into thinking it's time to sleep.

To see a total eclipse of the sun like this one, you have to be standing in just the right spot on Earth. It's important to wear special glasses to watch an eclipse of the sun. Looking directly at the sun can damage your eyes.

An eclipse of the sun lasts only a few minutes. An eclipse of the moon can last almost two hours.

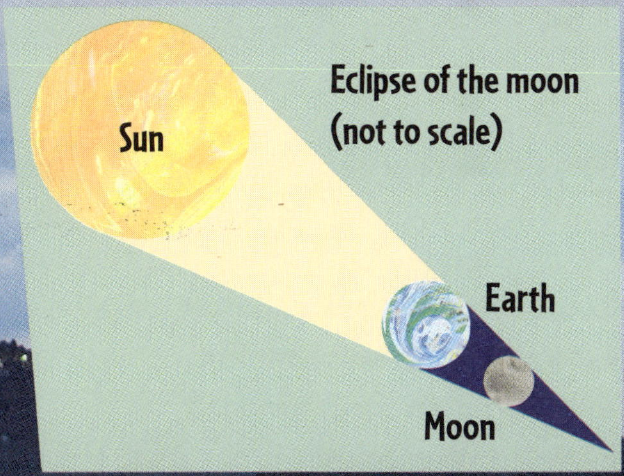

It takes about 45 minutes to put on a spacesuit. These suits come with a supply of oxygen and even water for the astronaut to drink.

Why do astronauts wear suits?

A spacesuit protects astronauts from the extreme hot and cold temperatures of space and provides oxygen for them to breathe. While astronauts are in a space station, they are safe from outside temperatures and they have air to breathe, so they can just wear their normal clothes. But sometimes they have to go outside for a spacewalk. That's when they put on these giant suits. Astronauts take spacewalks for different reasons: to do science experiments, to fix something or to test new equipment.

WACKY FACT

Astronauts can spend almost nine hours on a spacewalk, so they wear special astronaut nappies in case they need a wee!

Why don't we visit other planets?

Other planets, even the ones in our solar system, are really far away. We haven't yet built a spacecraft that can safely carry astronauts such long distances. Mars, one of our closest neighbours, is about 64 million kilometres away from us. That means the trip there and back would take almost two years, even in a rocket ship!

WACKY FACT

Humans haven't been to Mars yet, but six robotic rovers have explored the surface of the Red Planet.

Imagine what Mars could look like if humans lived there one day. Greenhouses would likely be needed to grow plants and food.

Mice get used to floating in a space station very quickly.

Why do we send animals to space?

One of the most important things astronauts do in space is conduct science experiments. They take lots of measurements of themselves to see how their bodies might have changed. They grow plants and care for animals, too. Working with animals helps scientists understand how living in space changes living things. In one experiment, astronauts collected mouse poo to find out if the good germs living in the mice's guts changed in space.

WHO KNOWS?

Scientists aren't sure if there is life on other planets, but they think it is likely, even though we haven't found it yet. When we do find life, it probably won't be human-like creatures with spaceships.

All kinds of animals have been to space, from chimpanzees to tardigrades like this one. Tardigrades are really tiny in real life – even smaller than an ant. This picture is enlarged.

Wow! What's that?

Here are some cosmic marvels. Can you match each one to its name?

Answers on page 271

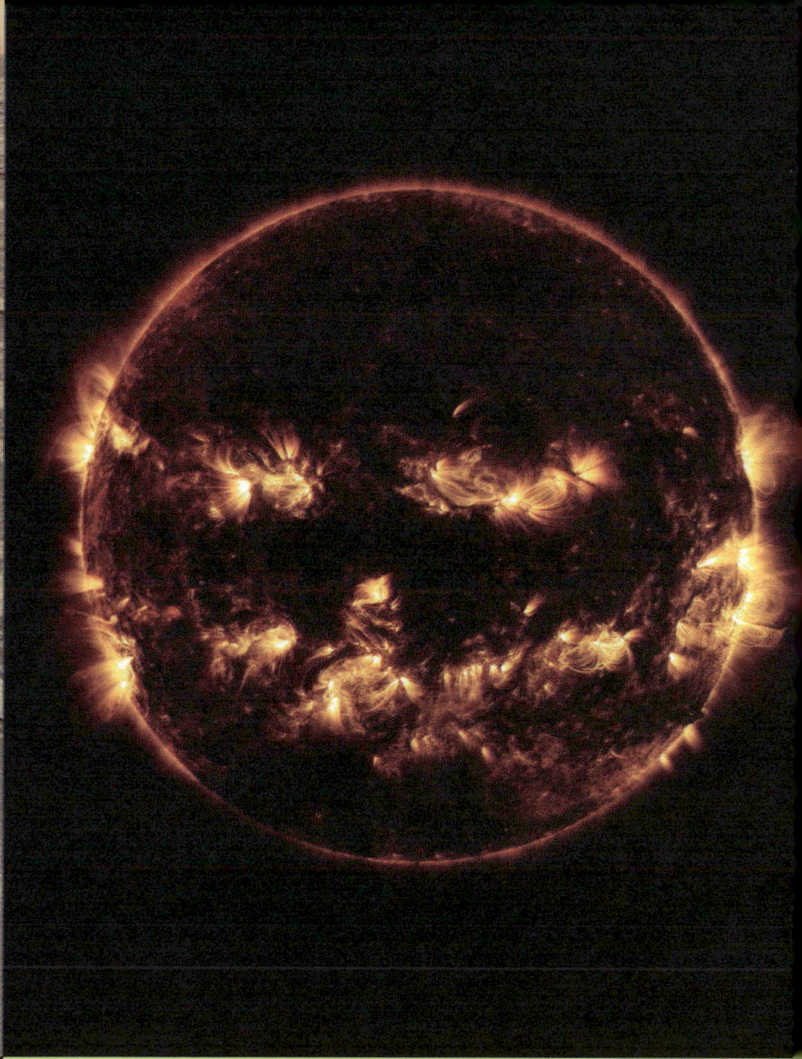

Artist's impression of a black hole

Footprint on the moon

Nebula cloud

Supernova

The sun

Mars rover

Glossary

absorb: To soak up.
angle: The direction from which a person or thing is approached.
atmosphere: The layer of gases that surrounds a planet.
axis: An imaginary line that an object rotates around. Earth's axis runs through its north and south poles.
bacteria: Very tiny living things that can be found in all natural environments on Earth, including on food and in the human body.
batter: A mixture of flour and liquid used for baking, as in a cake.
breed: A particular type of plant or animal. For example, a golden retriever is a breed of dog.
burrow: A hole or tunnel in the ground that an animal makes by digging.
cell: The tiny structure that makes up every living thing. Some living things, such as bacteria, are made of one cell, while others, such as humans, are made of trillions of cells.
chemical: What makes up any substance, whether solid, liquid or gas. Chlorine, water and gold are all chemicals.
chlorophyll: The green-coloured substance in plants that absorbs energy from light.
chrysalis: The hard, protective case that shelters a caterpillar while it turns into a moth or butterfly.
colony: A group of the same kind of animals that live and grow together, such as a bee colony.
crown: The part of a tooth that sticks out above the gum.
desert: An area of land that gets very little rain or snow each year.
diaphragm: A muscle that allows the lungs to draw air in and push it out.
eclipse: What happens when one object in space blocks another. For example, in an eclipse of the sun, the moon comes between Earth and the sun, blocking the sun from view.
electron: A very small particle with a negative charge. The movement of electrons creates electricity.
experiment: A trial or test made to find out about something.
extinction: The state of no longer existing.
follicle: A tiny pit in the skin through which hair grows.
fossil: The remains or traces of plants and animals that lived long ago.
freight: Goods or cargo carried by a ship, lorry, train or aeroplane.
gas: A substance, such as oxygen, that is mostly invisible and made of particles that flow around freely. Gas has no shape and fills the entire container that it is in, such as a balloon.
geode: A stone with a hollow space inside lined with crystals or minerals.
grasp: To seize and hold something.
gravity: A force of attraction that draws objects together.
harvest: The gathering of crops, such as corn or wheat.
herd: To keep or move animals together.
hibernate: To spend the winter in a state of rest.
inflatable: Possible to fill with a gas, such as air.
ingredient: One of the substances that make up a mixture.
intestines: Organs in the body shaped like long tubes that help break down food so the body can use it for energy.
joey: A baby marsupial, such as a kangaroo, wallaby or koala.
keratin: The substance that makes up hair, as well as horns, nails, hooves, beaks and feathers.
lava: Melted rock coming out of a volcano or crack on the surface of a rocky planet or moon.
larva: The young, wingless form of many insects, such as caterpillars and grubs, that hatches from an egg.
liquid: A substance, such as water, that can flow, and takes on the shape of the container it is poured into.
magma: Melted rock within a rocky planet or moon.
mammal: A warm-blooded animal that has a backbone, feeds its young with milk and has hair.
melanin: A substance that gives skin, hair and eyes their colour in humans and other animals.

microscope: A piece of equipment that uses one or more lenses to make something very small appear larger.
mineral: A solid substance that forms naturally, such as diamond or gold.
muscle: A body part that produces movement.
nimble: Quick and light when moving.
nocturnal: Active at night.
nutrient: A substance that helps plants and the bodies of people and animals work.
orbit: The route of an object in space, when it is travelling around a larger object under the influence of gravity.
organ: A body part that performs a function, such as the heart.
oxygen: A colourless, odourless, tasteless gas in the air that nearly all animals need to survive.
papillae: Small, rounded bumps on a part of the body.
particle: A tiny bit of matter, such as a molecule or atom.
planet: A natural round object that travels around a star in space.
plaque: A sticky, slimy substance made mostly of germs that builds up on teeth.
pollinator: Anything, such as a bee, that carries pollen from one flower to another so the plant can reproduce.
predator: An animal that kills and eats other animals.
pressure: How much one thing pushes against another thing.
prey: An animal that is killed and eaten by another animal.
reflective: A surface that is able to send back light.
ripe: When a fruit, vegetable or other food is ready to eat.
root: A part of a plant that is usually hidden underground.
saliva: A watery liquid in the mouth that moistens and breaks down chewed food.
seabed: The floor of the ocean.
self-defense: The act of defending yourself.
sensitive: To be very aware of how things feel, look, sound and smell.
skyscraper: A very tall building.
solar system: A star and the planets and other objects that travel around it.
solid: A substance that keeps its shape, such as a bowling ball or an ice cube.
space station: A human-made structure that travels around Earth and is where some astronauts live and work for a period of time.
species: A group of similar living things that are able to produce young with one another.
star: A huge, glowing ball of gases in space, such as the sun.
steam: The gas that water turns into when it is boiled.
swivel: To turn on a pivot, for example turning your head on your neck.
trot: To move at a pace between a walk and a run.
vehicle: Something used to move goods or people from one place to another.
venom: A poison produced by an animal (such as a snake or scorpion) and passed to the victim, usually by biting or stinging.
vibration: A very fast back-and-forth motion.
vortex: A spinning mass of air or fluid, as in a whirlpool.
warm-blooded: An animal that can make its own body heat, even when it is cold outside.
water vapour: Water in the form of gas, as in clouds or fog.
womb: An organ in most female mammals that holds and nourishes its unborn young.

Index

Source notes

This book's research process was multilayered. The authors used a wide range of reliable sources, and then fact-checkers used additional sources to verify the information. In addition, expert editors reviewed the chapters for accuracy (see page 270). The result is more sources than there is room to share here. Below is a sample of the authors' sources for each chapter.

General sources
bbc.com, bbc.co.uk; britannica.com; history.com; howstuffworks.com; livescience.com; nasa.gov; natgeokids.com; nationalgeographic.com; nature.com; newscientist.com; npr.org; sandiegozoo.org; scientificamerican.com; sciencedaily.com; sciencing.com; scijinks.gov; smithsonianmag.com; space.com; wonderopolis.org; woodlandtrust.org.uk

MINIBEASTS: **pp. 8–9** '10 Cool Facts About Ants!', natgeokids.com; 'Ant Architects: How Do Ants Construct Their Nests?', howitworksdaily.com; **pp. 10–11** 'Ask Smithsonian: How Do Spiders Make Their Webs?', smithsonianmag.com; 'What Are Spider Webs Made Of? And How Do They Spin Them?', nhm.ac.uk; **pp. 12–13** 'International Year of the Fly: Why Flies Are Important', bbc.co.uk; 'The Disgusting Reason You Should Never Eat Something a Fly Landed on', womansday.com; **pp. 14–15** 'How Many Legs Does a Millipede Really Have?', animals.howstuffworks.com; 'Centipede Facts for Kids', sciencing.com; **pp. 16–17** 'Where Do Honeybees Go in the Winter?', britannica.com; 'What Do Bees Do in Winter?', wonderopolis.org; '10 Facts About Honey Bees!', natgeokids.com; **pp. 18–19** '7-Spot Ladybird', woodlandtrust.org.uk; '10 Big Surprises About Ladybugs', rangerrick.org; 'Ladybird Facts!', natgeokids.com; **pp. 20–21** 'Plastic-Eating Caterpillar Could Munch Waste, Scientists Say', bbc.com; 'The Butterfly Life Cycle!', natgeokids.com; 'British Caterpillars: How to Identify 10 Common Species', woodlandtrust.org.uk; **pp. 22–23** 'Where Do Worms Go When the Ground Is Very Dry?', highlightskids.com; 'Earthworm', rspb.org.uk; **pp. 24–25** 'Slime-Fighting Slug Can Superglue Enemy Frogs to Trees for Days', newscientist.com; 'Why Do Snails Leave Slime Trails?', wonderopolis.org; 'Ask a Scientist: Why Are Slugs So Slimy?', carnegiemnh.org; **pp. 26–27** 'How Do Snails Get Their Shells?', animals.howstuffworks.com; 'Snails', ecospark.ca; **pp. 28–29** 'Mosquitoes: 20 Fun Facts About the Pesky Insects', cleveland.com; 'Useful Facts About Mosquitoes', orkin.com; 'Why Do Mosquitoes Bite Me and Not My Friend?', loc.gov; **pp. 30–31** '14 Fun Facts About Fireflies', smithsonianmag.com; '11 Cool Things You Never Knew About Fireflies', blogs.scientificamerican.com; 'Fireflies', nationalgeographic.com; **pp. 32–33** '11 Wondrous Facts About Praying Mantises', treehugger.com; 'The Bloodthirsty Truth of the Beautiful Orchid Mantis', discovermagazine.com; 'Praying Mantis', nationalgeographic.com; **pp. 34–35** 'When Twenty-Six Thousand Stinkbugs Invade Your Home', newyorker.com; 'Why Do Stink Bugs Stink?', news.ncsu.edu

PETS: **pp. 40–41** 'Why Do Dogs Sniff Each Other's Butts?', animals.howstuffworks.com; 'Why Dogs Sniff Each Other's Rear Ends', thesprucepets.com; 'Why Dogs Sniff Rear Ends', vcahospitals.com; **pp. 42–43** 'Why Do Cats Purr?', scientificamerican.com; '10 Fascinating Facts About Cats', purina.com; 'Why Do Cats Purr?', wonderopolis.org; **pp. 44–45** 'Clash of the Claws: Cats vs Dogs', howitworksdaily.com; '5 Reasons Cats Need Their Claws', parade.com; 'Claws vs Nails: What Do Dogs Have?', doghealth.com; **pp. 46–47** '10 Hopping Fun Rabbit Facts!', natgeokids.com; 'Facts About Rabbits', bluecross.org.uk; 'Why Do Rabbits Have Such Long Ears?', discoverwildlife.com; **pp. 48–49** 'What's the Difference Between a Turtle and a Tortoise?', britannica.com; 'Galápagos Tortoise', animals.sandiegozoo.org; 'Tortoise Adaptations: Lesson for Kids', study.com; **pp. 50–51** 'Your Hamster May Have Surprising Origins', nationalgeographic.com; 'Golden Hamster', britannica.com; **pp. 52–53** 'The Incredible Explosion of Dog Breeds', livescience.com; 'Why Are There More Different Types of Dogs Than There Are Cats?', wonderopolis.org; **pp. 54–55** 'How Fish Breathe', dkfindout.com; 'Our Favorite Facts About Animal Lungs', lung.org; 'How Do Fish Breathe Underwater?', wonderopolis.org; **pp. 56–57** 'Can Any Animals Talk and Use Language Like Humans?', bbc.co.uk; 'How Many Words Do Dogs Understand?', animals.howstuffworks.com; **pp. 58–59** 'How Do Whiskers Work?', discoverwildlife.com; 'Dr. Universe: Why Do Animals Have Whiskers?', askdruniverse.wsu.edu; **pp. 60–61** 'How Cat Tongues Work – and Can Inspire Human Tech', nationalgeographic.co.uk; 'How Do Cats Stay So Clean? Video Reveals Secrets of the Feline Tongue', sciencemag.org; 'Freaked Out By Your Cat's Scratchy Tongue? Don't Be! It's Keeping Them Cleaner', npr.org; **pp. 62–63** 'Squeaky Mice Reveal Emotion, Self-Expression in the Brain', scientificamerican.com; 'The Facial Expressions of Mice', sciencedaily.com; **pp. 64–65** 'What Can I Give My Gerbils to Chew On?', gerbilwelfare.com; 'Gerbils', rspca.org.uk; **pp. 66–67** 'To Shoe or Not to Shoe?', practicalhorsemanmag.com; 'H&H Question of the Week: To Shoe, or Not to Shoe – Should My Horse Go Barefoot?', horseandhound.co.uk; 'Horseshoe', britannica.com

WILD ANIMALS: **pp. 72–73** 'How Frogs Communicate', dkfindout.com; 'Loudest Frog in the World', bbc.co.uk; 'Frogs Use Their Lungs Like Noise-Canceling Headphones to Find Mates', sciencefocus.com; **pp. 74–75** 'Sharks Never Run Out of Teeth', scientificamerican.com; 'How Many Teeth Do Sharks Have?', wonderopolis.org; 'How Sharks Work', animals.howstuffworks.com; **pp. 76–77** 'Mystery Bumps', smithsonianmag.com; 'Crocodile Faces Are More Sensitive Than Human Fingertips', nationalgeographic.com; **pp. 78–79** 'Octopus Facts', natgeokids.com; 'Ten Curious Facts About Octopuses', smithsonianmag.com; **pp. 80–81** 'African Elephant', natgeokids.com; '10 Unforgettable Elephant Facts!', natgeokids.com; 'Top 10 Facts About Elephants', wwf.org.uk; **pp. 82–83** 'Kangaroo Facts', livescience.com;

'How Long Do Joeys Stay in the Pouch?', discoverwildlife.com; 'What's the Inside of a Kangaroo's Pouch Like?', sciencefocus.com; **pp. 84–85** 'How Birds Build Nests', rspb.org.uk; 'Birds' Nests', dkfindout.com; **pp. 86–87** '5 Things Friday: Your Questions Answered', gorillafund.org; 'Why Do Male Gorillas Beat Their Chests? New Study Offers Intriguing Evidence', nationalgeographic.com; **pp. 88–89** 'Why Does a Snake Flick Its Tongue?', livescience.com; 'Human Tongues Can Apparently Smell Things', livescience.com; **pp. 90–91** 'Why Are Flamingos Pink?', newscientist.com; 'Why Are Flamingos Pink?', bbc.co.uk; 'Why Are Flamingos Pink?', sciencefocus.com; **pp. 92–93** 'Squirrel', britannica.com; 'How Do Squirrels Remember Where They Buried Their Nuts?', livescience.com; 'Caching for Where and What: Evidence for a Mnemonic Strategy in a Scatter-Hoarder', royalsocietypublishing.org; **pp. 94–95** 'Bird's Eye View', nationalgeographic.org; 'Great Horned Owl', allaboutbirds.org; 'How Come Owls See at Night?', scienceline.ucsb.edu; **pp. 96–97** 'Why Do Giraffes Have Such Long Necks?', sciencefocus.com; 'Why Do Giraffes Have Long Necks?', wonderopolis.org; 'Giraffes Could Have Evolved Long Necks to Keep Cool', nature.com; **pp. 98–99** 'Why Did Penguins Stop Flying? The Answer Is Evolutionary', nationalgeographic.com; 'The Big Question: Why Can't Penguins Fly?', bbc.co.uk; 'Why Can't Penguins Fly?', wonderopolis.org

THE BODY: pp. 104–105 'Why Is Yawning So Contagious?', psychologytoday.com; 'Here's Why Yawns Are So Contagious', livescience.com; 'Once of Science's Most Baffling Questions? Why We Yawn', bbc.com; **pp. 106–107** 'Why Do Our Mouths Water?', livescience.com; 'What's Spit?', kidshealth.org; **pp. 108–109** 'Why Don't Baby Teeth Grow Up?', wonderopolis.org; 'When Do Baby Teeth Fall Out and Adult Teeth Come In?', healthline.com; **pp. 110–111** 'Why Do Some People Need Glasses?', wonderopolis.org; 'Why Do So Many Humans Need Glasses?', psychologytoday.com; **pp. 112–113** 'Why Do We Cry? The Science of Tears', independent.co.uk; 'Why Do Babies Cry So Much?', wonderopolis.org; **pp. 114–115** Walker, Matthew. *Why We Sleep: The New Science of Sleep and Dreams.* New York: Penguin, 2018; 'Dreams', sleepfoundation.org; 'What Does It Mean When We Dream?', medicalnewstoday.com; **pp. 116–117** 'Scientists Reveal the Real Reason You Have Eyelashes', latimes.com; 'Longer Eyelashes May Be Sexier but Not Always Better', nationalgeographic.com; **pp. 118–119** Bryson, Bill. *The Body: A Guide for Occupants.* New York: Doubleday, 2019; 'The Evolution of Skin Colors', psu.edu; 'Why Are People All Different Colors?', wonderopolis.org; **pp. 120–121** 'Taking Care of Your Teeth', kidshealth.org; 'When and How Often Should You Brush Your Teeth?', mayoclinic.org; **pp. 122–123** 'Why Do We Like to Dance – and Move to the Beat?', scientificamerican.com; 'The No. 1 Reason Music Has the Power to Make Us Feel Good', psychologytoday.com; **pp. 124–125** Enders, Giulia. *Gut: The Inside Story of Our Body's Most Underrated Organ.* Vancouver: Greystone Books, 2018; 'Why Does Your Stomach Growl When You Are Hungry?', scientificamerican.com; **pp. 126–127** 'Why Do We Hiccup?', medicalnewstoday.com; 'What Causes Hiccups?', kidshealth.org; 'Hiccups', mayoclinic.org; **pp. 128–129** 'What Kids Should Know About How Hair Grows', aad.org; 'Your Hair', kidshealth.org; **pp. 130–131** 'Why Do We Have Fingernails?', livescience.com; 'Curious Kids: Why Do We Have Fingernails and Toenails?', education.abc.net.au

FOOD: pp. 136–137 'Fruits, Nuts and Berries', dkfindout.com; 'What's the Difference Between a Fruit and a Vegetable?', recipes.howstuffworks.com; **pp. 138–139** 'Why We Love the Sweet Life', livescience.com; 'Sweet Tooth Surprise: 5 Things You May Not Know About Sugar', today.com; **pp. 140–141** 'Fungus vs Mold', sciencing.com; 'How Does Mold Grow on Food?', sciencing.com; 'Mold Terrarium', exploratorium.edu; **pp. 142–143** 'Why Does Chocolate Melt in Your Hand?', loc.gov; 'Chocolate Facts, Effects & History', livescience.com; **pp. 144–145** 'Why Does Chopping an Onion Make You Cry?', loc.gov; 'Origin and History of Onions', iosrjournals.org; **pp. 146–147** 'The Science Behind Why We Love Stinky Cheese', bonappetit.com; 'What Stinky Cheese Tells Us About the Science of Disgust', smithsonianmag.com; 'This Is Why Stinky Cheeses Stink', rd.com; **pp. 148–149** 'Why Are Chili Peppers So Spicy?', wonderopolis.org; 'Why Are Chillies So Hot?', news.bbc.co.uk; 'The Cool Science of Hot Peppers', sciencenewsforstudents.org; **pp. 150–151** 'How Does Popcorn Pop?', nal.usda.gov; 'Explore the 'Pop' in Popcorn', scientificamerican.com; 'Why Does Popcorn Pop?', childrensmuseum.org; **pp. 152–153** 'What Are Fruits & Vegetables That Grow Under the Ground?', sciencing.com; 'Root Vegetables: The Underground Garden', aces.illinois.edu; **pp. 154–155** 'The Science of Cake', theguardian.com; 'Tallest Cake', guinnessworldrecords.com; 'How Does Baking Powder Work in Cooking?', thoughtco.com; **pp. 156–157** 'What Causes Ice Cream Headache?', health.harvard.edu; 'Neuroscientists Explain How the Sensation of Brain Freeze Works', sciencedaily.com; **pp. 158–159** 'Ask a Grown-Up: Why Does Jelly Wobble?', theguardian.com; 'Why Does Jelly Wobble?', howitworksdaily.com; 'Why Does Jello Jiggle?', foodrepublic.com; **pp. 160–161** 'Why Do Bananas Turn Brown?', britannica.com; 'What Causes Banana Peels to Turn Brown?', scienceline.ucsb.edu; 'Why Do Bananas Go Brown and Ripen Other Fruit?', bbc.com; **pp. 162–163** 'What Are Raisins?', thespruceeats.com; 'Can You Unwrinkle a Raisin?', fivethirtyeight.com; 'Raisins in the Sun: Wrinkled Little Fruits Have Long History, Tasty Possibilities', deseret.com

HOW STUFF WORKS: pp. 168–169 'The Nose Cone Experts', nasa.gov; 'Rockets and Rocket Launches Explained', nationalgeographic.com; 'Rocket Nose Cones and Altitude', aerospaceweb.org; **pp. 170–171** 'Scientists Finally Have an Explanation for Why Helicopters Are So Loud', businessinsider.com; 'NASA Researcher Develops Model That

Could Quiet Down Noisy Helicopters', nasa.gov; **pp. 172–173** 'Meep Meep! The History and Evolution of Car Horns', caranddriver.com; 'Car Horns – A History', cogapa.com; **pp. 174–175** 'How Trains Work', science.howstuffworks.com; 'Why Do Trains Run on Tracks?', vpr.org; **pp. 176–177** 'A Short History of the Elevator', cnn.com; 'Who Invented the Elevator?', history.com; 'How Elevators Work', science.howstuffworks.com; **pp. 178–179** 'On Reflection: Eight Mysterious Facts About Mirrors', bbc.co.uk; 'Mirror Image: Reflection and Refraction of Light', livescience.com; 'Who's That Baby in the Mirror?', psychologytoday.com; **pp. 180–181** 'How to Keep a 1500-Foot Skyscraper from Falling Over', wired.com; 'How Skyscrapers Work', science.howstuffworks.com; **pp. 182–183** 'How Does a Garbage Truck Work?', itstillruns.com; 'Then and Now: A Look at How the Garbage Truck Has Evolved', waste360.com; **pp. 184–185** 'Why Do Batteries Go Flat?', sciencing.com; 'How Do Batteries Work?', qrg.northwestern.edu; **pp. 186–187** 'Why Do Jets Leave a White Trail in the Sky?', scientificamerican.com; 'Why Do Airplanes Leave Trails in the Sky?', travelandleisure.com; **pp. 188–189** 'Where Does All Our Poop Go?', livescience.com; 'How Toilets Work', explainthatstuff.com; **pp. 190–191** 'Buoyancy Testing: Will It Sink or Float?', scienceworksmuseum.org; 'How Does a Floating Plastic Duckie End Up Where It Does?', blogs.scientificamerican.com; **pp. 192–193** 'The Hidden Genius and Influence of the Traffic Light', wired.com; 'This Is Why Traffic Lights Are Red, Yellow and Green', rd.com; **pp. 194–195** 'The First Ice Skates Weren't for Jumps and Twirls – They Were for Getting Around', smothsonianmag.com; 'The Surprising Science of Why Ice Is So Slippery', vox.com

EARTH: pp. 200–201 'Why Do Earthquakes Happen?', geo.mtu.edu; 'The Science of Earthquakes', usgs.gov; 'What Is an Earthquake?', spaceplace.nasa.gov; **pp. 202–203** 'The Big Question: Why Do Volcanoes Erupt?', bbc.co.uk; 'How Do Volcanoes Erupt?', usgs.gov; '17 Explosive Volcano Facts!', natgeokids.com; **pp. 204–205** 'Why Does the Ocean Have Waves?', oceanservice.noaa.gov; 'Currents, Waves, and Tides', ocean.si.edu; **pp. 206–207** 'Here's What Happened the Day the Dinosaurs Died', nationalgeographic.com; 'These Are the Dinosaurs That Didn't Die', nationalgeographic.com; 'Dinosaur Facts', amnh.org; **pp. 208–209** 'How and Why Did Flower Color First Evolve?', realclearscience.com; 'What Flower Colours Do Birds and Bees Prefer?', abc.net.au; 'The Birds and the Bees', evolution.berkeley.edu; **pp. 210–211** 'Rainbow', nationalgeographic.org; 'What Causes a Rainbow?', scijinks.gov; 'Rainbows: How They Form & How to See Them', livescience.com; **pp. 212–213** 'Why Is the Sky Blue?', highlightskids.com; 'Why Is the Sky Blue?', spaceplace.nasa.gov; **pp. 214–215** 'What Causes Rain?', scijinks.gov; 'Why Does It Rain?', metoffice.gov.uk; 'The Water Cycle!', natgeokids.com; **pp. 216–217** 'Why Are Mountains So High?', earth.stanford.edu; 'Fold Mountain', nationalgeographic.org; 'How Are Mountains Made?', wonderopolis.org; **pp. 218–219** 'Science of Summer: Where Does Beach Sand Come From?', livescience.com; 'How Does Sand Form?', oceanservice.noaa.gov; 'Why Do Some Beaches Have Sand and Others Have Pebbles?', howitworksdaily.com; **pp. 220–221** 'Why Do Leaves Fall in Autumn?', britannica.com; 'Why Leaves Really Fall Off Trees', npr.org; **pp. 222–223** 'Facts About Geodes', sciencing.com; 'How Do Geodes Form?', fossilera.com; 'What Is a Geode?', wonderopolis.org; **pp. 224–225** 'Types of Clouds', scijinks.gov; 'Clouds and How They Form', scied.ucar.edu; 'Cloud Facts for Kids', sciencekids.co.nz; **pp. 226–227** 'Desert', nationalgeographic.org; 'Antarctica's Biggest Mysteries: Secrets of a Frozen World', livescience.com; 'The Sahara: Earth's Largest Hot Desert', livescience.com

SPACE: pp. 232–233 'Why Does the Universe Make So Many Tiny Stars?', astronomy.com; 'How Many Stars Are There in the Universe?', space.com; 'Stars – Facts and Information', nationalgeographic.com; **pp. 234–235** 'Why Do Stars Twinkle?', starchild.gsfc.nasa.gov; 'Top 10 Cool Things About Stars', earthsky.org; 'All About Stars', scholastic.com; **pp. 236–237** 'Why Does Outer Space Look Black?', livescience.com; 'Why Is Space Black?', starchild.gsfc.nasa.gov; **pp. 238–239** 'Why Does the Sun Shine?', earthsky.org; 'Earth's Sun: Facts About the Sun's Age, Size and History', space.com; **pp. 240–241** 'Why Are Planets Round?', spaceplace.nasa.gov; 'Is the Earth Round?', oceanservice.noaa.gov; **pp. 242–243** 'Why Is Mars Red?', space.com; 'Why Is Mars Red?', childrensmuseum.org; 'This Is Why Mars Is Red and Dead While Earth Is Blue and Alive', forbes.com; **pp. 244–245** 'Why Does Saturn Have Rings?', spaceplace.nasa.gov; 'Why Does Saturn Have Rings Around It?', livescience.com; 'Which Planets Have Rings?', universetoday.com; **pp. 246–247** 'Why So Blue? Neptune's Atmosphere and Color', solarsystem.nasa.gov; 'All About Neptune', spaceplace.nasa.gov; **pp. 248–249** 'Why Do We Have Day and Night?', astroedu.iau.org; 'Why Is There Day and Night?', starchild.gsfc.nasa.gov; **pp. 250–251** 'What Are the Moon's Phases?', spaceplace.nasa.gov; 'What Are the Phases of the Moon?', starchild.gsfc.nasa.gov; **pp. 252–253** 'What Is an Eclipse?', nasa.gov; 'Why Do Eclipses Happen?', astronomynow.com; **pp. 254–255** 'What Is a Spacesuit?', nasa.gov; 'What Is a Spacewalk?', nasa.gov; **pp. 256–257** 'Here's Why There's Still Not a Human on Mars', nationalgeographic.com; 'Curious Kids: Why Can't We Put People on Mars?', theconversation.com; **pp. 258–259** 'Why Do We Still Send Animals to Space?', livescience.com; 'Animals in Space', nasa.gov; 'Why Do We Send Animals to Space?', space.com

Picture credits

The publisher would like to thank the following for permission to reproduce their images. The publisher apologises for any omissions and will be pleased to make any corrections in future editions.

l = left; r = right; t = top; b = bottom; c = centre; u = upper

FRONT COVER: ult Martin Harvey/Getty Images; **ulc** hsvrs/iStock.com; **ulb** Butterfly Hunter/Shutterstock; **rct** David Herraez Calzada/Shutterstock; **rcb1** Yevgen Romanenko/Getty Images; **rcb2** Biitli/iStock.com; **rb** Vladi333/Shutterstock; **BINDING:** Juniors Bildarchiv GmbH/Alamy; **BACK COVER:** GlobalP/iStock.com; **CONTENTS: p. 4 t–b** Michael Nichols; Alena Ozerova/Shutterstock; Martin Harvey/Getty Images; StefaNikolic/Getty Images; **p. 5 t–b** subjug/iStock.com; Ian Littlewood/Alamy; T.w. Van Urk/Dreamstime.com; Jürgen Fälchle/Alamy; **MINIBEASTS: p. 7** Michael Nichols; **p. 8** The Jungle Explorer/Shutterstock; **p. 11** Stephen Dalton/Nature Picture Library; **p. 13** toos/iStock.com; **p. 14** Sing5pan/Shutterstock; **pp. 14–15** Anan Kaewkhammul/Shutterstock; **p. 15** Scruggelgreen/Dreamstime.com; **p. 17** rupbilder/AdobeStock.com; **pp. 18–19** Albert Visage/FLPA/Minden Pictures; **p. 19 r** Janny2/iStock.com; **p. 19 tc** blickwinkel/Alamy; **p. 19 bc** Genevieve Vallee/Alamy; **p. 19 tl** FloWBo/iStock.com; **p. 19 bl** GlobalP/iStock.com; **p. 21 b** Butterfly Hunter/Shutterstock; **p. 25** Oliver Eitge/Getty Images; **p. 28 l** MarcusVDT/Shutterstock; **p. 28 r** nechaevkon/Shutterstock; **p. 30–31** Diliana Nikolova/Alamy; **p. 32** Thomas Marent/Minden Pictures; **p. 33** GlobalP/iStock.com; **p. 35** Michael J. Raupp; **p. 36 tr** FC_Italy/Alamy; **p. 36 br** Artzone Creatives/Shutterstock; **p. 36 bl** Jason Ondreicka/iStock.com; **p.37 tr** Robert Pickett/Corbis/Getty Images; **p. 37 tl** BIOSPHOTO/Alamy; **p. 37 br** Jurgen Otto; **PETS: p. 39** Alena Ozerova/Shutterstock; **p. 40** Mark Taylor/NPL/Minden Pictures; **p. 42** Oleksandr Boiko/Dreamstime.com; **p. 43** Rembolle/Shutterstock; **p. 44** EkaterinaZakharova/iStock.com; **p. 45** Joe Blossom/Alamy; **p. 47** Picsguru/iStock.com; **p. 51** INSADCO Photography/Alamy; **p. 52 bl** Ivantsov/iStock.com; **p. 52–53** Eric Isselee/Shutterstock; **p. 53 br** Juniors Bildarchiv GmbH/Alamy; **p. 54** Piotr Naskrecki/Minden Pictures; **p. 56 bl** Ivonne Wierink/Dreamstime.com; **p. 56 tr** Juniors Bildarchiv GmbH/Alamy; **p. 57** LivingThroughTheLens/iStock.com; **p. 58** Sonsedska/iStock.com; **p. 60** Seregraff/ iStock.com; **p. 62** Liufuyu/iStock.com; **p. 65** Txpeter/iStock.com; **p. 66** Kostic Dusan/123RF.com; **p. 68 tr** Eric Isselee/Shutterstock; **p. 68 br** Domiciano Pablo Romero Franco/Dreamstime.com; **p. 68 bl** Farlap/Alamy; **p. 69 tr** Isselee/Dreamstime.com; **p. 69 tl** Martin Harvey/Getty Images; **p. 69 br** Isselee/Dreamstime.com; **WILD ANIMALS: pp. 70–71** Martin Harvey/Getty Images; **p. 72 l** IrinaK/Shutterstock; **p. 72 r** Nataliia K/Shutterstock; **pp. 74–75** Reinhar Dirscherl/Alamy; **p. 75** REUTERS/Alamy; **p. 76–77** image BROKER/Alamy; **p. 77** FVE MEDIA/Alamy; **p. 81** Richard Du Toit/Minden Pictures; **p. 82** Westend61/Getty Images; **p. 84** Sumio Harada/Minden Pictures; **p. 88** Heidi and Hans-Juergen Koch/Minden Pictures; **p. 89** Michael D. Kern/Nature Picture Library; **pp. 94–95** GlobalP/iStock.com; **pp. 96–97** Ingo Arndt/Nature Picture Library; **p. 100 tr** DEA/C. DANI I. JESKE/Getty Images; **p. 100 br** Michael Aw **p. 100 bl** Joel Sartore; **p. 101 tr** Velvetfish/iStock.com; **p. 101 tl** Suzi Eszterhas/Minden Pictures; **p. 101 br** Santonius Silaban/Alamy; **THE BODY: p. 103** StefaNikolic/Getty Images; **p. 104** Dorling Kindersley Ltd/Alamy; **p. 106 t** Svitlana Bezuhlova/Dreamstime.com; **p. 106 b** Aniko Hobel/Getty Images; **p. 109** Jack Sullivan/Alamy; **pp. 110–111** sam74100/iStock.com; **p. 112** kali9/iStock.com; **p. 113** malija/AdobeStock.com; **pp. 116–117** Cavan Images/Getty Images; **pp. 118–119** Karel Noppe/Dreamstime.com; **pp. 120–121** Wanuttapong suwannasilp/Alamy; **p. 125** Heather Chang/Shutterstock/Offset.com; **pp. 126–127** PeopleImages/iStock.com; **p. 128** MStudioImages/iStock.com; **p. 129 l** cathyhawkins/Getty Images; **p. 129 r** Mayur Kakade/Getty Images; **p. 130 t** Paulina Zarakowska/EyeEm/Getty Images; **p. 130 b** Paulina Zarakowska/EyeEm/Getty Images **p. 131** SergeyChayko/iStock.com; **p. 132 tr** Du Cane Medical Imaging/Science Photo Library; **p. 132 br** Sebastian Kaulitzki/123RF.com; **p. 132 bl** Scott Camazine/Alamy; **p. 133 tr** Mark_Kuiken/iStock.com; **p. 133 tl** Dinodia Photos/Alamy; **p. 133 br** Puwadol Jaturawutthichai/123RF.com; **FOOD: p. 135** subjug/iStock.com; **p. 136 t** Josef Mohyla/iStock.com; **p. 137 clockwise from top** Sawomir Elasko/123RF.com; s-cphoto/iStock.com; Yutthasart Yanakornsiri/Dreamstime.com; getsaraporn/iStock.com; Sawomir Elasko/123RF.com; Ovydyborets/Dreamstime.com; Sergey Kolesnikov/123RF.com; **p. 139** tan4ikk/123RF.com; **p. 140** Sinhyu/iStock.com; **p. 141** RapidEye/iStock.com; **p. 142** Deepak Sethi/iStock.com; **p. 144** PA Images/Alamy; **p. 145** Daisy Symes, Noah Jerome, model; **p. 146 l** Anatoliy Karlyuk/Shutterstock; **p. 146 r** Lew Robertson/Getty Images; **p. 147** Maram/Shutterstock; **p. 148 l** Torresigner/iStock.com; **p. 148 c** Only Fabrizio/Shutterstock; **p. 148 r** Maxim Tatarinov/123RF.com; **p. 150** ktsdesign/Shutterstock; **p. 151** Coffeemill/Shutterstock; **p. 152** julie deshaies/Shutterstock; **p. 155** AnjelaGr/iStock.com; **p. 156** FluxFactory/iStock.com; **p. 158** ac_bnphotos/iStock.com; **p. 159** Philip Kinsey /123RF.com; **p. 160 bl** nndanko/iStock.com; **p. 160 t** Nataly Studio/Shutterstock; **p. 162** narikan/Shutterstock; **p. 163** Tsai siyen/iStock.com; **p. 164 tr** Kovaleva_Ka/iStock.com; **p. 164 br** Johan Nilsson/Getty Images; **p. 164 bl** Enzo Lisi/123RF.com; **p. 165 tr** Olga Yastremska/123RF.com; **p. 165 tl** Arpad Radoczy/123RF.com; **p. 165 br** Lick Me I'm Delicious; **HOW STUFF WORKS: p. 167** Ian Littlewood/Alamy; **pp. 168–169** Russell Kord/Alamy; **p. 170** Adam Calaitzis/iStock; **p. 172** donatas1205/Shutterstock; **p. 173** Anthony Bliss/Sussexsportphotography.com, John Biggs (owner), Annie the Model A Ford, Richard and Jude Rimmer, Anne and Dan Russell, passengers; **p. 177** Wing Yau Au Yeong/Alamy; **p. 178** Maskot/Getty Images; **p. 179** Enigma/Alamy; **pp. 180–181** dblight/iStock.com; **p. 181** swissmediavision/iStock.com; **pp. 182–183** Africa Studio/Shutterstock; **p. 185** Ocusfocus/Dreamstime.com; **pp. 186–187** Isannes/iStock.com; **p. 188** Win Nondakowit/123RF.com; **p. 193** 2ndLookGraphics/iStock.com; **p. 195** imageBROKER/Alamy; **p. 196 tr** Kim Petersen/Alamy; **p. 196 br** Xinhua/Alamy; **p. 196 bl** Motoring Picture Library/Alamy; **p. 197 tr** Victoria/AdobeStock.com; **p. 197 tl** Charles Stirling (Diving)/Alamy; **p. 197 br** Bloomberg/Getty Images; **EARTH: pp. 198–199** kruwt/iStock.com; **pp. 200–201** Design Pics Inc/Alamy; **pp. 204–205** willyambradberry/123RF.com; **p. 207** Seth Wenig/AP/Shutterstock; **pp. 210–211** Lisa5201/iStock.com; **p. 217** Easyturn/iStock.com; **pp. 218–219** Javier Brosch/Shutterstock; **p. 219** Oleksandr Lytvynenko/123RF.com; **p. 220** Kichigin/iStock.com; **pp. 222–223** Jorge Guerrero/AFP/Getty Images; **p. 223** Dafinchi/iStock.com; **pp. 224–225** KuderM/iStock.com; **pp. 226–227** Paul Biris/Getty Images; **pp. 226** Kim in Cherl/Getty Images; **p. 228 tr** zorpink/iStock.com; **p. 228 br** Kichigin/Shutterstock; **p. 228 bl** Tanes Ngamsom/Shutterstock; **p. 229 tr** Beautiful landscape/Shutterstock; **p. 229 tl** ellepistock/Shutterstock; **p. 229 br** Hiroshi Ichikawa/Shutterstock; **SPACE: pp. 230–231** Jürgen Fälchle/Alamy; **pp. 234–235** NASA/ESA/STScl; **p. 237** Elen11/iStock.com; **pp. 238–239** NASA/SDO/Science Photo Library; **pp. 242–243** Digital Vision/Getty Images; **pp. 246–247** 3quarks/iStock.com; **pp. 248–249** Alex Bracho/EyeEm/Getty Images; **pp. 252–253** Robert Loe/Getty Images; **p. 254** Jürgen Fälchle/Alamy; **p. 257** Jose Luis Pelaez/Getty Images; **p. 259** Planetfelicity/Dreamstime.com; **p. 260 tr** NASA/ESA/Hubble Heritage Team/STScl/AURA; **p. 260 br** Edwin Aldrin/NASA; **p. 260 bl** Martin Capek/123RF; **p. 261 tr** NASA/GSFC/SDO; **p. 261 tl** NASA/JPL-Caltech/MSSS; **p. 261 bl** NASA/CXC/MIT/L.Lopez/NSF/NRAO/VLA

Meet the WHY team!

AUTHORS

Sally Symes worked for many years as a designer of children's books before turning her skills to writing them, too. Her collaborations with Nick Sharratt have won several awards, including The Educational Writers' Award for *Gooey, Chewy, Rumble, Plop*, and The Southampton Favourite Book to Share Award for *Something Beginning with Blue*. She wrote nine of the stories in Britannica's *5-Minute Really True Stories for Bedtime*. She works from a shed in Sussex, UK, accompanied by her grumpy cat.

Stephanie Warren Drimmer writes about science and nature for kids. Her books have explored everything from baby animals to the human brain to outer space. Some of her favourite titles are *Beneath the Waves*, about the fantastic diversity of ocean life, and *Surprising Stories Behind Everyday Stuff*, about the weird histories of objects from ketchup to Frisbees. Stephanie lives in Los Angeles, California, USA.

ILLUSTRATOR

Kate Slater grew up on a beautiful farm in deepest Staffordshire, UK, and studied illustration at Kingston University. Her children's books include *A Peek at Beaks, A is for Ant, The Birthday Crown, The Little Red Hen, ABC London* and *Magpie's Treasure*. She has created several large-scale installations and window displays, including a flock of 400 life-size birds for the National Trust's Farne Islands.

EXPERT CONSULTANTS

Erik Gregersen is Britannica's expert on astronomy and space exploration. He loves astronomy because there is always some new and astonishing discovery.

Melissa Petruzzello is Britannica's plant and environmental science expert. She loves photosynthesis and the incredible ways that plants and other photosynthesisers support nearly all life on our beautiful planet.

John P. Rafferty is Britannica's expert on Earth and Earth processes. He is amazed by how Earth and its living things continually affect and change one another.

Kara Rogers is Britannica's expert on biomedicine and human health and disease. She is fascinated by the many ways in which tiny molecules in human cells affect the brain and body.

Wow! What's that? answers

MINIBEASTS

Owl butterfly
Hawaiian happy-face spider
Blue damselfly
Swallowtail caterpillar
Man-faced stink bug
Peacock spider

PETS

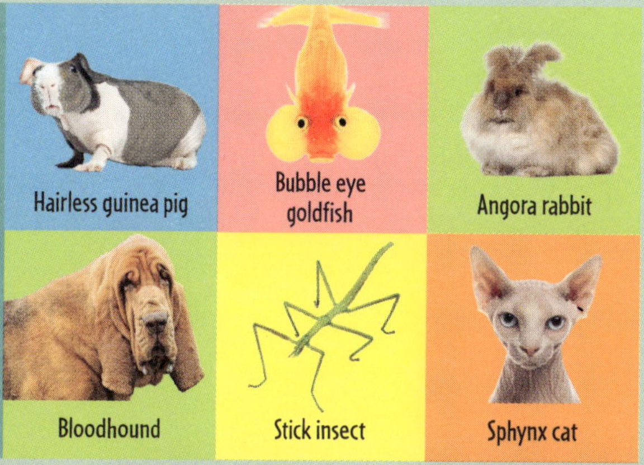

Hairless guinea pig
Bubble eye goldfish
Angora rabbit
Bloodhound
Stick insect
Sphynx cat

WILD ANIMALS

Thorny devil
Sloth
Peacock mantis shrimp
Tarsier
Dumbo octopus
Cassowary

THE BODY

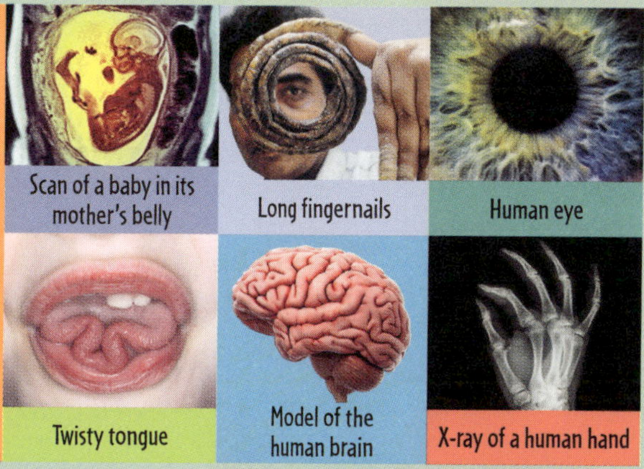

Scan of a baby in its mother's belly
Long fingernails
Human eye
Twisty tongue
Model of the human brain
X-ray of a human hand

FOOD

Dragon fruit
Romanesco broccoli
Whisked egg whites
Blue bananas
Casu marzu maggot-infested cheese
Glow-in-the-dark ice cream

HOW STUFF WORKS

Twisting skyscraper
Underwater scooter
Funhouse mirror
Bubble car
Outdoor lift
Gold-plated toilet

EARTH

Methuselah, the oldest tree in the world
Waterspout
Stalagmites and stalactites
Fossilised dinosaur footprint
Magnified snowflakes
Clouds on Mount Fuji, Japan

SPACE

Nebula cloud
Mars rover
The sun
Artist's impression of a black hole
Footprint on the moon
Supernova

BRITANNICA BOOKS

Britannica Books is an imprint of What on Earth Publishing,
published in collaboration with Britannica, Inc.
Allington Castle, Maidstone, Kent ME16 0NB, United Kingdom
30 Ridge Road Unit B, Greenbelt, Maryland, 20770, United States

First published in the United Kingdom in 2021

Picture credits on page 269.

Minibeasts, Pets, Wild Animals and The Body written by Sally Symes
Food, How Stuff Works, Earth and Space written by Stephanie Warren Drimmer
Illustrated by Kate Slater
Art directed and designed by Sally Symes
Edited by Priyanka Lamichhane
Picture research by Miriam Stein Battles and Sally Symes
Indexed by Connie Binder
Book production and print production by Booklabs.co.uk

Kate Slater has asserted her right to be identified as illustrator under the Copyright, Designs and Patents Act 1988.

Encyclopaedia Britannica: Alison Eldridge, Managing Editor; Erik Gregersen, Senior Editor, Astronomy and Space Exploration; Melissa Petruzzello, Assistant Editor of Plant and Environmental Science; John P. Rafferty, Editor, Earth and Life Sciences; Kara Rogers, Senior Editor, Biomedical Sciences; Michele Rita Metych, Fact Checking Supervisor

Britannica Books
Nancy Feresten, Publisher; Natalie Bellos, Executive Editor; Meg Osborne, Assistant Editor; Andy Forshaw, Art Director; Daisy Symes, Designer

A CIP catalogue record for this book is available from the British Library

ISBN: 978-93-5954-034-4

Published and Distributed in India by
Scholastic India Pvt. Ltd.

This Reprint Edition: October, 2025

Printed in India at : VK Global Digital Private Limited